STAGE & SCREEN
HAIRSTYLES

STAGE & SCREEN
HAIRSTYLES

A PRACTICAL REFERENCE FOR ACTORS, MODELS, HAIRSTYLISTS, PHOTOGRAPHERS, STAGE MANAGERS & DIRECTORS

Kit Spencer

WATSON-GUPTILL PUBLICATIONS / NEW YORK

First published in the United States in 2009 by
Watson-Guptill Publications, an imprint of the
Crown Publishing Group, a division of Random
House, Inc., New York
www.crownpublishing.com
www.watsonguptill.com

Library of Congress Catalog Card Number:
2008935963

ISBN-13: 978-0-8230-8497-5

QTT.PHA

Conceived, designed, and produced by
Quintet Publishing Limited
The Old Brewery
6 Blundell Street
London N7 9BH

Stylist and Makeup Artist: Kit Spencer
Photographer: Martin Norris
Picture research: Angela Levin, Kobal Collection
Designer: Ian Ascott
Art Editor: Michael Charles
Project Editor: Asha Savjani
Assistant Editor: Robert Davies
Proofreader: Rachel Connolly
Indexer: Vicki Robinson
Managing Editor: Donna Gregory
Publisher: James Tavendale

10 9 8 7 6 5 4 3 2 1

Printed in China by 1010 Printing International
Limited

CONTENTS

Foreword

Working on major films and television shows as a Hollywood Stylist, I am often asked what is the best approach to period hair. Through my own experience I have found that the key is really combining education and technique.

It is essential for every professional working in a visual medium like film, television, or photography, to be able to research the classic look of a period, define the style, and know which tools are needed in order to accomplish it. I often compare doing hairstyles for a period film to being an architect—first you have to design a blueprint and then you build it.

Whether creating a look for the science fiction universe of *Total Recall*, the military world of a prison camp in *Hart's War*, or the cowboys of the American West in *Tombstone*, I discovered that it was essential to know the techniques that create the hairstyles of each period. Each historical period is noted in this book's comprehensive guide, which is a great resource to begin to understand the basis for designing a style that is authentic.

During speaking engagements and interviews, industry professionals often approach me and ask how I go about the preparation for my work in film. For example, on *Interview with a Vampire*, I researched the history of the period in drawings and movie stills to establish an accurate hairstyle for the vampire Louis. The photo gallery in this book catalogs the hairstyles for a wide range of historical periods . In recreating the hairstyles for the period of 1970s San Francisco in the feature film *Milk*, for example, I used film archives and photographs from many different resources. Looking at movie stills allowed me to see what other hairstylists

were doing back in that decade. In order
to achieve the look that the director
wanted, I had to duplicate the
techniques and use the
tools from that time,
which this book also
illustrates for you.

   After thirty years of
working as a Hollywood
Stylist, I have created
a number of memorable
styles for both movies and
television. A book like this,
which describes the history and
techniques of period hair, should be on
the shelf in every professional hair and
makeup person's collection.

Michael White

Michael White, Motion Picture and
Television Hairstylist

🔘 How to use this book

This book is divided into 3 sections: Equipment and Techniques, the Gallery, and the Looks.

EQUIPMENT AND TECHNIQUES

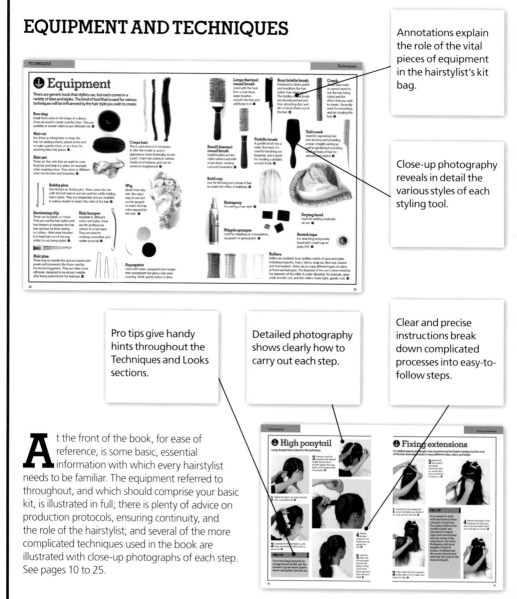

Annotations explain the role of the vital pieces of equipment in the hairstylist's kit bag.

Close-up photography reveals in detail the various styles of each styling tool.

Pro tips give handy hints throughout the Techniques and Looks sections.

Detailed photography shows clearly how to carry out each step.

Clear and precise instructions break down complicated processes into easy-to-follow steps.

At the front of the book, for ease of reference, is some basic, essential information with which every hairstylist needs to be familiar. The equipment referred to throughout, and which should comprise your basic kit, is illustrated in full; there is plenty of advice on production protocols, ensuring continuity, and the role of the hairstylist; and several of the more complicated techniques used in the book are illustrated with close-up photographs of each step. See pages 10 to 25.

THE GALLERY

From Hollywood movies to fringe theater, the worlds of studio, stage, and screen are fascinated with period productions. The drama and romance of historic settings have made for some memorable productions, which have often tested the shows' hairstylists to their limits. The art of period styling is showcased in this section, with images of iconic styles—mainly modeled by actors performing in movies set in the more distant past—as well as original photographs of classic hairstyles from recent history. This gallery of period looks, both original and recreated, is the inspiration for the next section. See pages 26 to 53.

A main look is selected for each period, to be recreated in the Looks section.

The period is described in terms of aesthetics and tastes and trends in hair styling.

The main look from the Gallery is blown up full page so you can see exactly what is being recreated.

A list of any unusual equipment you will need, in addition to the main elements of the hairstylist's kit bag, is included.

THE LOOKS

This is the main body of the book: step-by-step instructions, accompanied by detailed photographs, showing you how to recreate fifty period hairstyles. In each case, inspiration is drawn from one of the images featured in this section. The text is accompanied by pro tips, which introduce you to the secrets of the professional stylist—providing hints and information that will make life on set immeasurably easier. Each look lists the key equipment that you will need in addition to the key materials in every stylist's kit bag. For some very old looks, pottery and carvings are probably the only pictorial reference points available to stylists today. See pages 54 to 253.

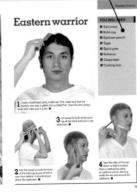

Introduction

There are various elements at work on set or backstage. The experienced stylist will have developed their own way of doing things and every scenario will be slightly different—some basic guidelines are outlined below.

Production protocols and paperwork

Within a production company you will have an Executive Producer, Series Producer, Producer, Production Manager, and Production Co-ordinator. Director, Lighting, Makeup, and Camera Operators are classified as crew and are hired on a freelance basis. The Line Producer or Production Manager is therefore the initial point of contact for the production and is responsible for hiring and firing. They will contact you to

check your availability for the shooting dates, negotiate rates, and finalize the terms of your contract. Once you have been confirmed for the job you will be asked to submit an estimated budget for the hairstyling department, including both materials and staff.

If you are working on a drama or film you will initially be sent a schedule, script, and the actors' pictures and details from the production office. A scene breakdown will be provided by a continuity person.

For all types of production, contact details will be exchanged with the Production Co-ordinator who will, prior to the production, send everyone a comprehensive contact list and daily call sheets for each day of the production once filming has begun.

The call sheet is your guide for each day of filming. It will contain the times you need to be at work and the expected time you will finish, details of the location, and health and safety notes. Before the production starts, you will be asked for your input to estimate the time it will take for each person in hair. These times will be worked into the overall timeline for the day and included in the call sheet.

Script breakdown, shooting schedules, and continuity

Once you have received the script, you will need to break it down into the characters, days, and then scenes. Using continuity sheets, begin to develop a filing system for the hairstyling department, perhaps having one file containing the character sheets in alphabetical order, and one file divided into shooting days and scenes containing a duplicate of the sheets for each character in those scenes.

You will then need to meet with the Director and Costume Designer to discuss the looks for each character. They will already have an idea of how they would like each character to look but will be keen to have your input and hear any ideas you may have. The Costume Designer will have prepared mood boards for each character and you will be able to reference them when designing the hair.

Once you have been given pictures of actors, file them with the relevant continuity sheets and make notes of your initial ideas. It is then advisable to talk to the actors themselves to get their input on how they feel their character should

the continuity sheets, to anyone in the hair department who will be working with that particular character so they can create the required look.

When shooting begins, a picture should be taken of each actor in each scene and placed in the relevant place in the continuity folder.

Safety and sanitation on set

The call sheet will outline the safety details for each day, highlighting any specific safety issues at the location. If you're shooting outdoors, the expected weather conditions will be outlined and you should ensure you dress appropriately. When on set, common sense should prevail—there will be lots of cables, kit boxes, overhead lights, and moving cameras.

You should ensure all your electrical items are working correctly and are regularly safety tested.

After each use any hair caught in brushes and combs should be removed and hairbrushes and combs should be washed regularly.

look. If the schedule allows it is advisable to meet with the actors to do a hair test as this will allow any difficulties or differences of opinion to be ironed out before shooting begins. It will also allow you to better estimate hair time required and ensure you don't overrun on

the first day. Actors may also need to change their hair color or length. Once the hair has been decided upon, take a picture of the actor and attach it to the continuity sheet.

Before shooting begins, you should create and label a hair bag for each character, which contains the styling products and hair accessories required to create their agreed look. These can then be passed, along with

Purchasing for production

Once you know the hair requirements for each character you can begin to estimate the costs involved. You will have been given a guideline of the available budget and, taking this into account along with the requirements, you will have an idea of what is affordable. You will then be able to begin to make purchasing decisions and decide how best to spend your budget. Good-quality wigs are expensive but cheaper wigs can look unrealistic. Renting may be the best option—work out the number of days the piece will be required for and the total rental costs and make a comparison with purchasing. Commissioning a wig to be made is the most expensive option as it is a highly skilled and lengthy process. Laying on crepe hair mustaches and beards will cost a fraction of the price of buying pieces knotted on lace, but it can be time-consuming and requires practice.

Stage differences

The role of the hairstylist differs slightly depending on the medium in which you are working. When an actor is performing in front of a camera, be it for film or television, a member of the hair team will be on hand throughout the filming for continuity checks, to ensure that the hair has not changed at all.

When an actor is working on the stage, however, it is more than likely that they will do their own hair, as they will have been taught to do as part of their drama school training. The look they create will have been designed by a professional stylist beforehand, and they will have been taught before the run begins exactly how to recreate the looks required for the show.

13

⚙ Equipment

There are generic tools that stylists use, but each comes in a variety of sizes and styles. The kind of tool that is used for various techniques will be influenced by the hairstyle you wish to create.

Bun ring
Made from nylon in the shape of a donut, these are used to create a perfect bun. They are available in several colors to suit different hair. ➡

Hair rat
Also known as a "hair pad," use these as a tube to wrap the hair, for adding volume, joined at the end to make a perfect bun, or as a base for attaching false hair pieces. ➡

Hair net
These are fine nets that are used to cover long hair and keep it in place, for example when wearing a bun. They come in different colors for blondes and brunettes. ➡

Crepe hair
This is used when it is necessary to alter the model or actor's appearance more drastically, to suit a part. Crepe hair comes in various shades and textures, and can be curled or straightened. ⬆

Bobby pins
Also known as "Kirby grips," these came into use with the bob haircut and are used for subtly holding hair in place. They are inexpensive and are available in various shades to match the color of the hair. ➡

Rollers
Rollers are available in an endless variety of sizes and styles, including magnetic, foam, Velcro, snap-on, flexi-rod, heated and non-heated—there are as many different types of rollers as there are hairstyles. The final size of the curl is determined by the diameter of the roller. A wider diameter, for example, gives a full, smooth curl, and thin rollers create tight, spirally curls. ⬆

Sectioning clip
These can be plastic or metal. They are used by hairstylists and hairdressers to separate the hair into sections for blow-drying or cutting—their main function is to keep hair out of the way while it is not being styled. ⬇

Hair bungee
Available in different colors and styles, these are the professional version of a hair band. They are used for creating a smoother and neater ponytail. ➡

Hairpins
These may be needlelike and encrusted with jewels and ornaments like those used by the ancient Egyptians. They are often more utilitarian, designed to be almost invisible after being inserted into the hairstyle. ➡

Curling iron
Also known as "curling tongs," these are used for curling the hair. These come with various barrel widths. ➡

Large thermal round brush
Used with the heat from a hairdryer, larger brushes smooth the hair and add body to it. ↩

Ponytail brush
Used to gather the hair neatly and firmly into a ponytail. ↩

Comb
These have wide or narrow teeth to suit the hair being styled and the effect that you wish to create. Generally used for smoothing and detangling the hair. ↩

Tail comb
Used for separating hair into sections and providing a neat, straight part as well as gently backcombing small sections of hair for volume and control. →

Small thermal round brush
Small brushes act like rollers when used with a hairdryer, creating curl and movement. →

Paddle brush
A paddle brush has a wide, flat head. It is used for brushing out long hair, and is good for creating a straight, smooth finish. →

Bald cap
Used for blocking out a head of hair to create the effect of baldness. →

Drying hood
Used for setting a hairstyle on set. ↑

Aquapaint
Used with water, aquapaint lasts longer than greasepaint but gives a less even covering. Work quickly before it dries. ↑

Stipple sponges
Used for stippling on a foundation, aquapaint, or greasepaint. ↩

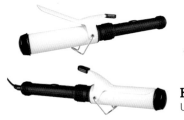

Hair straighteners
Used on dry hair to straighten it. ↑

Hairdryer
Used for drying the hair. ↑

Basic styling

Before styling hair for blowdrying and straightening, divide it into sections and clip them out of the way.

Sectioning

1 Starting on top of the head in the middle, lift a section by dividing with a tail comb. ⬇

2 Comb through. ⬇

5 Use small clips for small sections, and larger clips for bigger sections. ➡

3 Twist hair, and loop onto itself so it sits on top of the roots of the hairs in the section, then clip. ⬆

4 Work around the crown then in rows down the head. ⬆

Blow-drying

1 Hair should be spritzed through with a water spray and thoroughly combed. ⬇

2 Section the hair into small, manageable pieces, and hold with sectioning clips. ⬇

3 Starting at the back, just above the neck, unclip the hair. Apply styling product if necessary and work into the hair. ⬇

4 Choose an appropriate round blow-drying brush for the length of hair. The longer the hair, the bigger the brush. ⬆

5 Brush the hair over the top of the brush and begin to dry. First lift the hair directly upward and dry the root from underneath for lift then angle the hairdryer down the shaft of the hair. Slowly move the dryer and the brush toward the ends of the hair, drying it from above. ⬅

6 Rest the hair on the arm of the hairdryer and reposition the brush underneath and repeat drying from above. Once the hair is dry, unclip the next section and repeat the drying process. As you move toward the top of the head, give the hair more root lift. ⬆

Straightening hair

1 Section the hair. ⬇

2 Starting at the bottom at the back of the head, unclip a section of hair. ⬅

3 Spritz with heat protection spray. ➡

4 Run straighteners through from root to ends. ⬅

🔘 Heat styling

There are various methods for heat styling dry hair—these are the basic methods that you will use.

Heated rollers

1 The direction in which heated rollers are placed on the head, and the size of rollers used, will be dictated by the final desired style—it is known as the "pli." Section the hair accordingly using a tail comb. ⬆

2 Roll sectioned hair onto the rollers. The amount of hair rolled onto each depends on the size of the roller. When the roller is sitting against the scalp the space it occupies should be equivalent to the hair that has been rolled onto it. ⬆

3 Pin the rollers in place. They should be as hot as possible, and allowed to cool on the head for as long as possible. Remove the rollers. ⬇

4 Once they have been taken out, the hair can either be combed out and set into place, or the curls can be lightly shaken out for a more natural look. You can also tease the ends. ⬇

Crimping

1 Unclip a section of hair, and comb through. ⬇

2 Take pre-heated crimpers, and hold down on the hair at the top, close to the hair shaft. Hold for ten seconds, and release. ⬇

Curling with irons

1 Spritz hair with heat protecting spray. ⬇

2 Starting at the nape of the neck, unclip a section of hair, and comb through. ⬆

3 Move down the hair to the end. ⬆

3 Wrap the section of hair around the pre-heated curling iron from the root (not the ends) until you get to the end. Close the arm of the iron over the end of the hair. ⬆

4 Loosen by combing through with your fingers, and leave for a ringlet effect or tease with a comb for more volume. ⬅

4 Separate the hair with the fingers, and lightly spray to hold. ⬆

High ponytail

Long, straight hair is ideal for this technique.

1 Gather the hair in one hand. Smooth with a ponytail brush. ⬆

2 Gradually lift the hair higher up the head, smoothing it with a brush as you do so. ⬆

3 Once you have the ponytail at the desired height and the hair is smooth against the scalp, hook a hair bungee under the ponytail. ➡

4 Pull the bungee away from the head and wrap around the hair. ⬆

5 Hook the other end of the bungee into the hair. Spray to finish and smooth down any loose hairs with your hand. ↩

PRO TIP

For a very high ponytail on a long-haired model, get the model to tip her head upside down and gather the hair up.

⚙ Fixing extensions

For added volume and length, hair extensions can be fixed in sections to the roots of the hair. Extensions come in many different sizes, colors, and styles.

3 Backcomb the model's hair lightly where the clips sit, so that they have something to attach to. ➔

1 Section the hair horizontally across the head, two-thirds of the way up from the root. ➊

PRO TIP

It is easiest to work with sections cut from a length of real hair, the same width as the model's head, pre-attached to toupee clips that are stitched into the seam of the extensions. For extra thickness, add more lengths of hair in layers, working from the crown downward, and trim the ends to the desired length.

4 Stretch the length of hair, and push the clips back down into the backcombed area, and style as normal. ⊙

2 Color match the hair extension to the color of the model's hair. Open the clips. ➊

❶ Attaching small sections

2 Clip out of the way. ⬇

3 Hold the seam against the section part. ⬆

1 Lift the hair above where you're attaching the extra section. ⬆

4 Clip the extra section of hair into place using two bobby pins crossed in an "X" shape. ⬅

5 Unclip the hair above the section, and comb through. ➡

❷ Braiding

2 Divide the section into three equal parts. ⬇

3 Cross the outer portion over the middle one. Work down the hair, taking one outside portion at a time and crossing over the middle. ⬅

1 Take the section of hair that you want to braid and clip it out of the way. ⬆

PRO TIP

Keep the pressure even on both sides as you are braiding, so that the braid is even from the top to the bottom.

4 Secure at the bottom with a clear, snag-free hair band. ➡

⚙ Making a fake bun

Bun rings are very versatile and are a key structural device in hairstyling. They can have a number of roles, and making a perfect bun is just one of them.

1 Cut open a bun ring and measure a length of hair twice as long as the opened ring. ◑

3 Roll the ring onto the hair, asking someone else to hold the ends of the hair so that you get a good, tight roll. ◒

4 Secure with bobby pins to keep the hair taut. Smooth down any loose strands and spray with hairspray to set. Fix in place. ◑

2 Stitch a sewn section of real hair onto the bun ring, doubling it up so that it is thick. ◑

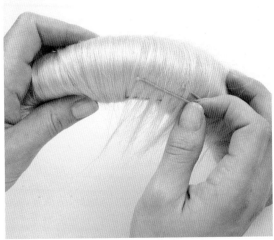

PRO TIP

If cut open, bun rings should always be slightly shorter than the length of hair.

⚉ Making ringlets

It is unlikely that your model will always have perfect length hair for the part, and fake hair (real and crepe) will be a necessary part of your kit. Making ringlets from sections of real hair for a period look is simple to do but very effective.

1 Make ringlets using a sewn strip of real hair in the same color as the model's own hair. Make eight strips, each 1½ inches long. ⬇

2 Tightly wrap the strips, one by one, around the smallest-barreled curling iron available to you. Clamp tightly and hold for thirty seconds. ➡

3 Once curled, spray each strip to set the shape and snip off loose ends. Release from the iron by sliding off carefully and fix in place. ➡

PRO TIP

Ask someone to help you as two pairs of hands are best for this.

⚙ Backcombing

Backcombing is used to create a variety of effects, but the basic technique is similar. Backcombing is also known as "teasing." The roots are backcombed to add height or volume as in the beehive style demonstrated below.

2 Backcomb from the middle of the hair down to the root, pushing the hair gently. Once you've finished teasing a section of hair, allow it to fall forward. ⬇

1 Working from front to back, lift a section of hair where you want the height to begin. Comb the section through. ⬆

3 Take the next section behind this and do the same thing. ⬆

4 Allow the hair to fall forward and repeat. Spray with hairspray to set. ⬅

5 Flop the hair back and let it drop. Smooth over with a comb. ⬇

PRO TIP

Sit the model on a low chair when carrying out this technique.

The number of sections you do will depend on how much volume you want and where.

THE

GALLERY

Introduction

The Gallery section (pages 29 to 53) is the red carpet of this book, on which actors and actresses strut their stuff dressed as characters from across the ages. The looks illustrated on these pages have been chosen for authenticity and their faithfulness to the period of history that they depict, as well as for their color and dramatic impact. When recreating period looks, Hollywood has had a tendency, in the past, to come to its own conclusions about how people wore their hair and did their makeup, and different periods have often been misrepresented in film and on television sets because of this. Makeup and dress have been tailored to suit the tastes of modern-day audiences, who would not take to the portrayal of different looks in the same way that contemporary audiences might have done. This is something that hairstylists have to bear in mind when they are asked to recreate a certain look on set. They must be accurate in their representation of the styles from different periods, and they must attempt to be faithful to history. But the hairstylist also has the task of creating a look that will evoke the personality of their character in the mind of their audience. With these various elements at play, a main look has been selected for each of the periods featured in this gallery, and these have been reproduced in clear and comprehensive steps, along with illustrations, on pages 54 to 253.

🔵 Prehistoric

250,000 BCE–3,200 BCE

For obvious reasons, the hairstyle used when recreating a Stone Age setting is shaggy and unkempt. In the early days of cinema, prehistoric characters were often given a tidy, trimmed appearance; now they are much more heavily styled to appear ragged and dirty.

⊕ *Skullduggery*, 1969

⊕ **John Lone,** *Iceman*, 1984, see page 54

⊕ **Robin Williams,** *Being Human*, 1993

⊕ **Everett Mcgill,** *Quest For Fire*, 1981

🔵 Biblical

1450 BCE–95 CE

The Old Testament of the Bible implies that for men, long hair is a sign of virility and strength: Samson, along with other ancient Israelites, proudly wore his hair long—a custom maintained to this day by Orthodox Jews. Women in biblical times also seem to have opted for long hair in flowing styles.

⊕ **Ted Neeley,** *Jesus Christ Superstar*, 1973

⊕ **Richard Gere,** *King David*, 1985, see page 58

⊕ **Ava Gardner,** *The Bible*, 1965

⊕ **Charlton Heston,** *The Ten Commandments*, 1956

 Ancient Greece

1100 BCE–140 BCE

Women of the classical period wore their hair very long, allowing it to fall loosely over their shoulders—though later, it was often fastened with a headband. Slaves—or freeborn women in mourning—kept their hair short.

⊕ **Diane Kruger,** *Troy*, 2004

⊕ **Angelina Jolie, Val Kilmer, Colin Farrell,** *Alexander*, 2004, see page 62

⊕ **Ursula Andress,** *Clash of The Titans*, 1980

⊕ **Brad Pitt,** *Troy*, 2004

Ancient Rome

30 BCE–400 CE

Young Roman women usually wore their hair simply coiled into a knot on top of their head; but married women preferred ornate styles, sometimes using a soap made of tallow and ashes to dye their hair a yellowish red. Men kept their hair short and were usually clean-shaven: the tonsor, or barber, was a skilled and well-paid professional.

⊕ **Jean Simmons,** *The Robe*, 1953

⊕ **Deborah Kerr,** *Quo Vadis*, 1951, see page 66

⊕ **Joaquin Phoenix,** *Gladiator*, 2000

⊕ **Connie Nielsen,** *Gladiator*, 2000

🔅 Mayan girl

250 CE–900 CE

Hairstyles signified rank in ancient South American society, with common men cutting the hair on their forehead and leaving the rest to grow. Warrior-class men had a shock of hair on the left-hand side of the head. Women left their hair uncut and unbound, tying it only on special occasions.

🌐 *Apocalypto*, 2006

🌐 *Apocalypto*, 2006, see page 70

🌐 **Dalia Hernandez, Rudy Youngblood,** *Apocalypto*, 2006

🌐 *Apocalypto*, 2006

🔅 Eastern warrior

1200 CE–1400 CE

Hair was a symbol of strength and honor for a warrior. The Mongols believed that hairstyles should resemble the wings of an eagle. Men shaved the sides of the top of the head, leaving the back hair long and braiding it. Women wore the hair pulled away from the face, decorating it with strings of felt.

🌐 **Patrick Gallagher,** *Night At The Museum,* 2006

🌐 **Yul Brynner,** *Taras Bulba,* 1962, see page 74

🌐 **Tadanobu Asano,** *Mongol,* 2007

🌐 **Zhang Ziyi,** *Musa,* 2005

🌐 Celtic warrior

1300–1350

Celtic warriors smeared their long hair with quicklime or a resin-based gel, and pulled it back from the forehead. Beards, too, were worn long. Closely shorn hair was a sign of slavery or a mark of punishment.

⊕ Mel Gibson, *Braveheart,* 1995, see page 78

⊕ Catherine McCormack, Mel Gibson, *Braveheart,* 1995

⊕ *Braveheart,* 1995

⊕ Catherine McCormack, Mel Gibson, *Braveheart,* 1995

🌐 Italian Renaissance

1450–1600

Renaissance society allowed more freedom in dress and other fashions than had previously been the norm, and headdresses revealed more hair than in previous centuries. Portraits by Titian, the Venetian painter, popularized a red-blonde color that rich Italian women attempted to emulate by dying their hair with a mixture of coppery-red pigments.

⊕ Valentina Cervi, *Artemisia,* 1997, see page 82

⊕ Jeremy Irons, *The Merchant of Venice,* 2004

⊕ Olivia Hussey, *Romeo and Juliet,* 1968

⊕ Gabriel Gabrio, *Lucretia Borgia,* 1935

Elizabethan England

1560–1600

Queen Elizabeth's red hair was the object of envy and the color was copied by many aristocratic women. The starched ruffs often worn in this period led to upswept styles, often arranged over a wire frame in a heart shape.

Samantha Morton, *Elizabeth: The Golden Age,* 2007, see page 86

Colin Firth, Judi Dench, *Shakespeare In Love,* 1998

Clive Owen, *Elizabeth: The Golden Age,* 2007

Cate Blanchett, *Elizabeth: The Golden Age,* 2007

Restoration

1660–1690

Luxurious hairstyles abounded in the restored court of Charles II of England. Thick, flowing ringlets were common in both men and women, representing a liberation from the severe and puritanical styles that had been *de rigueur* in the brief years of the Republic.

Alec Guinness, *Cromwell,* 1970, see page 90

Sir Cedric Hardwicke, *Nell Gwyn,* 1934

Kim Novak, *The Amorous Adventures of Moll Flanders,* 1965

Linda Darnell, *Forever Amber,* 1947

33

18th-century France (man)

1700–1800

Rich men usually wore wigs, which were close to the scalp with the main part of the hair brushed backward. From around 1715, the wigs were often powdered, especially for formal occasions. Some men wore a pigtail wrapped in black fabric, a style made popular by Prussian soldiers.

Dustin Hoffman, *Perfume: The Story of a Murderer,* 2006, see page 94

John Malkovich, *Dangerous Liaisons,* 1988

Nick Nolte, Greta Scacchi, *Jefferson in Paris,* 1995

Simon Callow, Greta Scacchi, *Jefferson In Paris,* 1995

18th-century France (woman)

1700–1800

Close-to-the-head styles were common until around 1760, when the coiffure became raised and more elaborate, with the aid of hair pads and pomade—a waxy styling substance made from apples and lard. In the 1780s there was a particular vogue for wearing huge hats perched on the already high hair.

Lena Olin, *Casanova,* 2005, see page 98

Jean-Paul Belmondo, Odile Versois, *Cartouche,* 1961

Glenn Close, *Dangerous Liaisons,* 1988

Mira Sorvino, *Triumph of Love,* 2001

🔵 Regency England

1715–1835

The dramatic, high hairstyles and horsehair wigs of the Georgian period gave way, around the beginning of the nineteenth century, to a softer Regency look—of the kind most familiar today from Jane Austen adaptations. Men stopped wearing wigs and kept their own hair short. Women wore their hair up and fastened the bun with bonnets, ribbons, and—for the rich—jeweled diadems.

🔵 **Rhys Ifans,** *Vanity Fair*, 2004

🔵 **Frances Dee,** *Becky Sharp*, 1935, see page 102

🔵 **Matthew Macfadyen, Simon Woods,** *Pride and Prejudice*, 2005

🔵 **Greer Garson, Laurence Olivier,** *Pride and Prejudice*, 1940

🔵 Imperial Russia

1720–1917

Subjects of the Russian empire were segregated into nobility, clergy, merchants, cossacks, and peasants. The nobility could afford to spend a lot of money on their appearance, and for women the look was well-groomed with volume on the top of the head, and gentle curls framing the face. In 1910, Diaghilev's *Ballet Russes* began to be influential in aristocratic fashion.

🔵 **Greta Garbo,** *Anna Karenina*, 1935

🔵 **Audrey Hepburn,** *War and Peace*, 1956, see page 106

🔵 **Greta Garbo,** *Anna Karenina*, 1935

🔵 **Anita Ekberg,** *War and Peace*, 1956

☗ French aristocracy

1750–1795

This period saw fashion reach heights of fantasy and abundant ornamentation in Europe, especially among the French aristocracy. Extreme hairstyles were commonplace, as were wigs, which were built up high on the head, powdered, and adorned with decorative objects. By the 1780s, a country-inspired fashion had taken over and hats worn over a mass of natural-colored curls replaced these elaborate hairstyles.

⊕ **Dolores Del Rio,** *Madame du Barry,* 1934

⊕ **Norma Shearer,** *Marie Antoinette,* 1938, see page 110

⊕ **Simon Baker,** *The Affair of the Necklace,* 2001

⊕ **Jason Schwartzman, Kirsten Dunst,** *Marie Antoinette,* 2006

☗ French Revolution

1789–1799

Under the influence of Jean-Jacques Rousseau and British tailoring, and as a reaction against the lavish excess of the Louis XVI years, a long-simmering movement toward simplicity and democratization of dress began to triumph over the fashion of eighteenth-century France. Many had their heads chopped off, and with them their adorned hair and powdered wigs. The period was followed by one of austerity.

⊕ **John Malkovich,** *Dangerous Liaisons,* 1988

⊕ **Glenn Close, John Malkovich,** *Dangerous Liaisons,* 1988, see page 114

⊕ **Rachel Hurd-Wood,** *Perfume: The Story of a Murderer,* 2006

⊕ **Lillian Gish, Dorothy Gish,** *Orphans of the Storm,* 1922

🌀 Pirate

1800–1900

The long-haired, tousled look which we associate with pirates was not a choice: in humid Mediterranean and Caribbean climates, keeping the hair short and clean while shipboard would have been impossible. Since Johnny Depp's first performance as Jack Sparrow in 2003, beading and braiding in the hair have been added to the typical look.

⊕ Johnny Depp, *Pirates of the Caribbean: Dead Man's Chest,* 2006, see page 118

⊕ Dustin Hoffman, *Hook,* 1991

⊕ Peter Ustinov, *Blackbeard's Ghost,* 1968

⊕ Jean Peters, *Anne of the Indies,* 1951

🌀 Wild-west girl

1800–1970

The frontierswoman Calamity Jane and sharpshooting Annie Oakley have given us the typical image of the nineteenth-century cowgirl: shoulder-length hair tied in pigtails, combined with a healthy, suntanned complexion.

⊕ Jane Fonda, portrait, 1965, see page 122

⊕ Doris Day, *Calamity Jane,* 1953

⊕ Ella Raines, *Tall in the Saddle,* 1944

⊕ Grace Kelly, portrait, 1952

⊕ Napoleonic

1805–1815

Following the severities of the French Revolution, wealth and power began to rise—and hairstyles became more glamorous to match. Josephine, Napoleon's wife, set the style, with her passion for jewelry and adornment. Women had sleek hairstyles with jeweled diadems. Napoleon's own hair was cut close in the style called *le petit tondu*—the little crop.

⊕ Harvey Keitel, *The Duellists*, 1977, see page 126

⊕ Paul Bettany, *Master and Commander: The Far Side of the World*, 2003

⊕ John Neville, *Adventures of Gerard*, 1970

⊕ Virginia Mayo, *Captain Horatio Hornblower*, 1951

⊕ Victorian gentleman

1840–1900

Men kept their hair very short, dressing it into place with macassar oil, though they often had thick, bushy sideburns and beards. Curled hair was particularly fashionable in the 1830s and 40s, with the fashion later in the century tending toward the smooth and straight.

⊕ Ewan McGregor, Renee Zellweger, *Miss Potter*, 2006, see page 130

⊕ Robert Shaw, *Young Guns*, 1988

⊕ Charles Laughton, *The Barretts of Wimpole Street*, 1934

⊕ Basil Rathbone, *David Copperfield*, 1935

🔘 Victorian matriarch

1840–1900

Queen Victoria was strongly influenced by the French revolution, and when she lost her happiness with the death of her beloved husband Albert, she went into a period of mourning that influenced the clothing and hairstyles of the mid-eighteenth century all over the world. Mature women wore their hair up in an austere bun on the back of their heads, and when out of the house it was usual to cover the hair with a bonnet or hat.

⊕ Judi Dench, *Waste*, 1985, see page 134

⊕ Judi Dench, *The Importance of Being Earnest*, 2002

⊕ Irene Dunn, *The Mudlark*, 1950

⊕ Ava Gardner, *Fifty-five Days in Peking*, 1962

🔘 Upper-class Victorian lady

1840–1900

Only girls and very young women wore their hair down. Early- and mid-Victorian girls had very loose hair, but the fashion slowly changed to neater, more tightly packed curls.

⊕ Julianne Moore, *An Ideal Husband*, 1998, see page 138

⊕ Anna Neagle, *Victoria the Great*, 1937

⊕ Norma Shearer, *The Barretts of Wimpole Street*, 1934

⊕ Ingrid Bergman, *Gaslight*, 1944

⚙ Poor Victorian

1840–1900

In spite of the difficulty of keeping it clean, poor Victorian women often had long tresses of hair—except for the very poorest, who cut and sold their hair; and those in the workhouses, who were compelled to have their hair cropped.

⊕ **Jack Wild,** *Oliver!*, 1968

⊕ **Helena Bonham Carter,** *Sweeney Todd*, 2007, see page 142

⊕ **George C. Scott,** *A Christmas Carol*, 1984

⊕ **Freddie Jones,** *The Elephant Man*, 1980

⚙ US Civil War soldier

1861–1865

Neither the Union nor Confederate armies organized a barber service during the Civil War—so soldiers either arranged for their own haircut and shave, or went without. This is why the hair of the period was so often long and unkempt.

⊕ *The Red Badge of Courage*, 1951

⊕ **Jeff Daniels,** *Gettysburg*, 1993, see page 146

⊕ **Sam Elliott,** *Gettysburg*, 1993

⊕ **Denzel Washington,** *Glory*, 1989

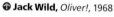

⚜ US Civil War lady

1861–1865

By far the most popular style was to have the hair arranged very low on the crown of the head, and wider to the sides. The hair was parted down the center and slicked down at the crown, then pulled back and secured into a bun. Younger women would sometimes drop the bun into a roll at the nape of the neck. Extra volume was added at the sides by using a "rat" of hair collected from the woman's hairbrush.

⊕ **Vivien Leigh,** *Gone with the Wind*, 1939, see page 150

⊕ **Winona Ryder,** *Little Women*, 1994

⊕ **Olivia De Havilland,** *Gone with the Wind*, 1939

⊕ **Renee Zellweger, Nicole Kidman,** *Cold Mountain*, 2003

⚜ Native American

1870–1930

Native American hairstyles differed from tribe to tribe, but the most familiar style today is the roach—usually known as the Mohawk or Mohican, after the two tribes who wore it most frequently. Native American men often wore artificial roaches, made of brightly dyed deer or porcupine hair.

⊕ **Hugh O'Brian,** *Seminole*, 1952, see page 154

⊕ **Cameron Mitchell,** *Pony Soldier*, 1952

⊕ **Linda Darnell,** *Buffalo Bill*, 1944

⊕ **Graham Greene,** *Dances with Wolves*, 1990

 Geisha

1900–2000

Geisha hairstyles have varied throughout history, but the most recognized style is worn high, tied into sections with string and adorned with haircombs. Many modern geisha use wigs in their professional lives, while maiko use their natural hair. Both must be regularly tended by highly skilled artisans, but traditional hairstyling is a slowly dying art.

⊕ **Sylvia Sidney,** *Madame Butterfly*, 1932, see page 158

⊕ **Daigoro Tachibana,** *Zatoichi*, 2003

⊕ **Shirley MacLaine,** *My Geisha*, 1962

⊕ **Lucy Liu,** *Charlie's Angels*, 2000

 Edwardian

1901–1910

The full, soft style of the women of this period was often helped by the use of pads of false hair. This gave the appearance of luxuriant, long tresses, caught up on the head. Hair frames called the Marie Stuart were worn to help style the hair into an attractive heart shape, recalling the styles of Elizabethan England.

⊕ **Billy Zane, Kate Winslet,** *Titanic*, 1997, see page 162

⊕ **Bernard Cribbins,** *The Railway Children*, 1970

⊕ **Julie Andrews,** *Mary Poppins*, 1964

⊕ **Hugh Grant,** *Maurice*, 1988

🔆 America's sweetheart

1913–1950

Mary Pickford was an early Hollywood star and also a movie pioneer—she became a film producer, and was the first actress to earn more than a million dollars per year. Her superstar status made hers the style to be copied from around 1917 to the mid 1920s, with her trademark curls becoming a symbol of the virtuous American woman.

⊕ **Mary Pickford,** 1917, see page 166

⊕ **Mary Pickford,** portrait

⊕ **Lillian Gish,** portrait

⊕ **Alice Terry, Rudolph Valentino,** *The Four Horsemen of the Apocalypse*, 1921

🔆 Jazz-age flapper

1918–1929

Short, sleek hair was a key part of the flapper style which emerged in the mid-1920s. Boyish cuts, such as the bob and the Eton crop, were worn—part of the general flapper trend toward reducing the femininity of their appearance.

⊕ **Clara Bow,** portrait, 1926, see page 170

⊕ **Betty Balfour,** portrait, 1924

⊕ **Catherine Zeta-Jones,** *Chicago*, 2002

⊕ **Marilyn Monroe,** *Some Like it Hot*, 1959

1930s depression

1929–1939

The economic depression meant that the 1930s were an age of hardship across America and Europe. The classic cinematic image of the period is of a hobo—a shabbily dressed, downtrodden traveler, looking for work. To recreate this look, the hair needs to be short, wavy, and dirty.

⊕ **Barbara Pepper, Tom Keene, Karen Morley,** *Our Daily Bread*, 1934

⊕ **William Powell,** *My Man Godfrey*, 1936, see page 174

⊕ **Dorris Bowden, Henry Fonda,** *The Grapes of Wrath*, 1940

⊕ **John Turturro, Tim Blake Nelson, George Clooney,** *O Brother, Where Art Thou?*, 2000

🕒 1930s Hollywood starlet

1930–1939

No one celebrity epitomizes the golden age of Hollywood as well as Bette Davis. Her string of exceptional performances in Warner Brothers' movies made her one of the most imitated icons of her time. Her soft, wavy, golden hair was crucial to Davis's look—though perhaps less so than her famously distinctive eyes.

⊕ **Bette Davis,** portrait, *c.*1932, see page 178

⊕ **Jean Harlow,** portrait, 1934

⊕ **Marlene Dietrich,** portrait, 1936

⊕ **Greta Garbo,** portrait, 1932

⚫ 1930s leading man

1930–1939

The 1930s were a decade of elegance and sophistication, partly as a reaction against the flamboyant styles of the 1920s. Men wore a shirt and tie and very rarely went outside without a hat or cap. Hair was a very important element in this respectable, clean look. It was worn quite short and slicked down with a side part—going to the barber was a regular occurence in the life of a 1930s leading man.

⊕ **Cary Grant,** portrait, 1930s

⊕ **Errol Flynn,** portrait, c.1939, see page 182

⊕ **Clark Gable,** portrait, 1934

⊕ **Robert Mitchum,** portrait, 1930s

⚫ WWII forces' sweetheart

1939–1945

Betty Grable's platinum blonde hair was widely envied by her rival pin-up girls across the globe. At the same time, the idea of the forces' sweetheart was born, and many young women were likely to have a much more girl-next-door image: Patricia Roc and Gracie Fields were among the entertainers whose glamour was less overt.

⊕ **Patricia Roc,** *Millions Like Us,* 1943

⊕ **Betty Grable,** portrait, see page 186

⊕ **Gloria De Haven,** portrait, 1944

⊕ **Judy Garland,** *For Me and My Gal,* 1942

● WWII soldier

1939–1945

Neat, short, slicked-back hair is the emblem of the military officer from this period. Soldiers from the lower ranks, then as now, were more likely to sport a crew cut—an even, very short trim all over the head, made with an electric razor. This style evolved into the flattop in the late 1940s and early 1950s: a crew-cut back and sides with short hair standing in a flat block shape on top of the head.

⊕ **Montgomery Clift,** *The Search*, 1948

⊕ **Ralph Fiennes,** *Schindler's List*, 1993, see page 190

⊕ **Montgomery Clift,** portrait, 1950

⊕ **James McAvoy,** *Atonement*, 2007

● 1940s glamour

1940–1949

A side part and rolls of hair were the key aspects of the 1940s look. The pins holding elaborate curls in place were always very carefully hidden. Hollywood actresses had perfect hair, but in reality women's hair would have been noticeably frizzy, as curling iron at this time had no temperature control.

⊕ **Veronica Lake,** portrait, 1943

⊕ **Scarlett Johansson,** *The Black Dahlia*, 2006, see page 194

⊕ **Lauren Bacall,** portrait, 1943

⊕ **Rita Hayworth,** portrait, 1948

⚙ Gangster chic

1940–1980

Gangster films developed from the shocking stories and sensational headlines of the Great Depression. Often troubled characters, real-life gangsters earned a living by becoming feared and respected in their neighborhoods. Short, flawlessly slicked back hair helped them to paint a fearsome picture of someone who was cold and emotionally detached.

⊕ **Al Pacino,** *The Godfather Part II*, 1974, see page 198

⊕ **Ray Liotta, Robert De Niro, Paul Sorvino, Joe Pesci,** *Goodfellas*, 1990

⊕ **Humphrey Bogart,** *High Sierra*, 1941

⊕ **Richard Widmark,** *Kiss of Death*, 1947

⚙ Blonde bombshell

1950–1959

Marilyn Monroe's bleached-blonde pin curls were essential to her era-defining sexy-yet-innocent style, which inspired dozens of photographers and portraitists. This style is easiest to recreate if you already have loose curls or waves; otherwise the curling can be a lengthy process.

⊕ **Jayne Mansfield,** portrait, 1950s, see page 202

⊕ **Mamie Van Doren,** portrait, 1956

⊕ **Marilyn Monroe,** portrait, 1950s

⊕ **Sheree North,** portrait, 1950s

 # 1950s flip

1950–1959

At the end of the 1950s, the flip became a sought-after style for sophisticated women. Originating with Mary Tyler Moore, who appeared on the *Dick van Dyke Show*, the style's popularity was reinforced by international style icons such as the Italian actress Sophia Loren, and Grace Kelly, who became Princess of Monaco from 1956.

⊕ **Sophia Loren,** portrait, 1965

⊕ **Joanne Woodward,** portrait, 1960, see page 206

⊕ **Grace Kelly,** portrait, 1956

⊕ **Joanne Woodward,** portrait,1960

1950s housewife

1950–1959

Golden hair with a slight curl, pinned up in a bun or chignon, helps to create the look of the idealized 1950s housewife: feminine, maternal, and content with her lot. Lucille Ball—star of *I Love Lucy*, the most-watched US TV series of its time—helped to define the style.

⊕ **Ginger Rogers,** portrait, 1950s

⊕ **Doris Day,** portrait, 1957, see page 210

⊕ **Lucille Ball, Desi Arnaz,** *I Love Lucy* (US TV series), 1951–1957

⊕ **Doris Day,** portrait, 1952

1950s glamour

1950–1959

In these pre-blowdryer days, an arduous process of pinning and curling was necessary to achieve the softly curling style popularized by stars such as Elizabeth Taylor and Sandra Dee. Many women kept their rollers in while they slept to maximize the effect; and large amounts of lacquer were needed to fix every fashionable style in place.

Audrey Hepburn, portrait, 1953

Elizabeth Taylor, *portrait,* 1954

Ava Gardner, portrait, 1952, see page 214

Grace Kelly, portrait, 1954

Rock 'n' roll

1950–1965

Rebels and nonconformists everywhere in the 60s opted for the duck's tail—the hair combed back around the side of the head, with a center part running from the crown to the nape of the neck. Hollywood stylists seized on this style as a way of representing the increasingly wild youth of their time; and in the UK, this was the haircut of choice for Rockers and Teddy Boys.

Warren Beatty, portrait, 1961, see page 226

David Hemmings, portrait, 1966

Michael Caine, *The Italian Job,* 1969

Dustin Hoffman, portrait, 1967

⊕ 1960s chick

1960–1965

The beehive style reigned supreme in the first half of the 1960s. Elaborately teased and generously lacquered, the beehive was the height of chic after Audrey Hepburn wore this style in *Breakfast at Tiffany's*. Not everyone was so fond of the style—some calling it the B-52, because it resembles the bulbous nose of a B-52 bomber jet.

⊕ **Brittany Snow,** *Hairspray,* 2007, see page 218

⊕ **Faye Dunaway,** portrait, 1967

⊕ **Nicole Blonsky**, *Hairspray,* 2007

⊕ **Julie Andrews,** portrait, 1966

⊕ Swinging sixties

1960–1969

Sixties hair was achieved through suffering, with women sleeping in coke-can sized rollers night after night or, if they had a hot date, sitting under loud, monster hairdryers for an hour beforehand. Volume was the aim, and big curls fluffed up and combed into waves epitomized the look.

⊕ **Veruschka,** *Blow Up,* 1966, see page 222

⊕ **Michelle Pfeiffer,** *Grease II,* 1982

⊕ **Anika Noni Rose, Beyonce Knowles, Jennifer Hudson,** *Dreamgirls,* 2006

⊕ **Heather Graham,** *Austin Powers: The Spy Who Shagged Me,* 1999

🎱 1970s disco

1970–1979

The tousled style that Farrah Fawcett adopted for her role in the TV series *Charlie's Angels* became an international trend in the mid-1970s when the influence of psychedelics and the hippie movement advocated a natural look for men and women. Many African-Americans rejected white-influenced styles such as the "conk" and adopted the afro as a sign of black pride.

🔘 **Pam Dawber,** portrait, 1978

🔘 **Farrah Fawcett,** *Charlie's Angels* (US TV series), 1976–1981, see page 230

🔘 **Tamara Dobson,** *Cleopatra Jones*, 1973

🔘 **Susan Dey,** *The Partridge Family* (US TV series), 1970–1974

🎱 1980s power dressing

1980–1989

Oversized shoulder pads were mirrored by the dramatic hairstyles popular among successful women in business, politics, and culture. Busy people opted for styles that could be quickly blow-dried and curled with electric curling iron rather than heated rollers.

🔘 **Melanie Griffith,** *Working Girl*, 1988

🔘 **Morgan Fairchild,** portrait, c.1980, see page 234

🔘 **Kim Cattrall,** *Mannequin*, 1987

🔘 **Katey Sagal,** *Married with Children* (US TV series), 1987–1997

1980s men's fashion

1980–1989

The mullet—short top and sides with long hair at the back—first became popular with young men in the late 1970s, due in large part to glam rock musician David Bowie. Its popularity peaked in the 1980s, with musicians like Phil Collins and actors such as Richard Dean Anderson (star of the hit US TV series *MacGyver*) sporting the look for years.

⊕ **David Hasselhoff,** *Baywatch* (US TV series), 1989–2001

⊕ **Patrick Swayze,** 1988, see page 238

⊕ **Matthew Broderick,** *Ferris Bueller's Day Off*, 1986

⊕ **Val Kilmer,** *Top Gun*, 1986

1980s girls' fashion

1980–1989

A variety of relatively extreme styles were popular. Excessively crimped hair was in vogue in the middle of the decade, the modern crimping iron having been invented in 1972. The feathered style worn by Heather Locklear in *Dynasty* was widely copied; and glam-rock-style long hair also had its devotees.

⊕ **Michelle Pfeiffer,** *Scarface*, 1983

⊕ **Madonna,** *Desperately Seeking Susan*, 1985, see page 242

⊕ **Daryl Hannah,** *Splash*, 1984

⊕ **Cher,** *Moonstruck*, 1987

🔅 1990s glamour

1990–2005

The glamour icons of the early 1990s were models like Cindy Crawford; but from 1995, rising star Jennifer Aniston became the most emulated star, with her "Rachel" look—named after the character Aniston played in *Friends*—becoming the most-requested cut in America and Europe.

⊕ **Jennifer Aniston,** portrait, c.2005, see page 246

⊕ **Meg Ryan,** *You've Got Mail,* 1998

⊕ **Sandra Bullock,** portrait, 1991

⊕ **Heather Locklear,** portrait, 1992

🔅 1990s grunge

1990–1995

Grunge, emerging in the early 1990s, was a key part of the 1990s anti-fashion trend. Gray, khaki, or olive-colored clothes were partnered with straggly hairstyles, covering much of the face. An iconic figure was the unkempt singer Kurt Cobain, described by one music journalist as "just too lazy to shampoo."

⊕ **Matthew Fox,** *Party of Five* (US TV series), 1994–2000, see page 250

⊕ **Brad Pitt,** portrait, 1993

⊕ **Winona Ryder,** *Reality Bites,* 1994

⊕ **Adam Sandler, Brendan Fraser, Steve Buscemi,** *Airheads,* 1994

Prehistoric

1 Use your hands to find a natural part in the hair and make a rough and messy look. ⬆

2 Spray with water. ⬆

3 Gently clench sections of hair in your hand one at a time to separate the different sections so the hair falls naturally. ⬆

4 Spray with gel spray to set and to create a sticky surface. ⬆

5 Apply stage dirt by lightly sprinkling it onto the hair. ⬇

PRO TIP

If you find the hair is getting too out of control, use a comb to put it back into place. Don't rake the comb through the hair, just lightly run it over the top to keep the layers.

Biblical

- ➔ Sectioning clips
- ➔ Styling lotion
- ➔ Crepe hair
- ➔ Tail comb
- ➔ Curling iron

1 Divide hair into small sections all over the head—this makes it easier to work with. ➔

2 Spray through with styling lotion.

3 Starting at the nape of the neck, unclip one section at a time and iron the hair all over. ➔

59

4 Prepare some long lengths of crepe hair, divide into two, and braid into a third length of the model's own hair. With the point of a tail comb, lift a section of hair about an inch above the ears on either side of the head and clip out of the way. Start a braid with the actual hair and weave the crepe hair into it. ➡

5 Unclip the hair and loosen it with your fingers. ⬇

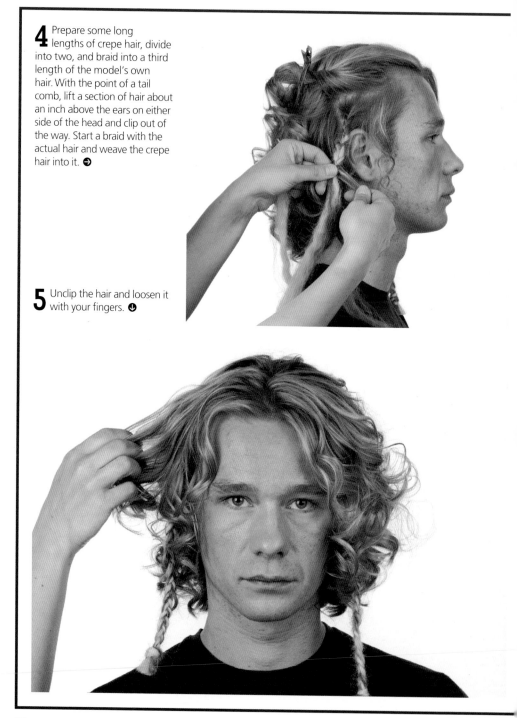

PRO TIP

Be careful with hair products—use just enough to give you the style you want (you can always add more). Otherwise, it will weigh the hair down, causing it to lose its definition.

Ancient Greece

1 Separate the front section— from the middle of the left ear to the middle of the right ear—from the rest of the hair, and clip it out of the way. ➔

2 Divide the back section of the hair horizontally into four parts. Put the middle two sections into ponytails using hair bands. Separate the front sections into twists using sectioning clips. Spray all over with styling tonic. ➔

5 Pin the curls in the two ponytails to the back of the head. Pin the top ones to the crown, above the base of the top ponytail, leaving the bottom ones loose. ➔

3 Curl the top ponytail using a small-barreled curling iron (see page 19). ↑

6 Unclip the front sections down and place the tiara on the head, securing the two arms of the tiara with bobby pins. ↓

4 Curl the lower and any loose hair with the iron to obtain loose corkscrew curls. ↑

7 Iron the front section of hair. ⬆

8 Using hairpins, pin the curls that are loose at the front into the back section, lifting it over the tiara. Don't pull the curls tight. ⬆

9 Fix with hairspray. ⬇

PRO TIP

When pinning the hair, use bobby pins for structural support and hairpins to anchor the hair into its final shape for styling.

Ancient Rome

YOU WILL NEED

- ➔ Hair bands
- ➔ Sectioning clips
- ➔ Curling iron or hair wand
- ➔ Bobby pins
- ➔ Comb
- ➔ Large bristle brush
- ➔ Ribbon
- ➔ Artificial flowers

1 Separate the front section of the hair, from ear to ear and clip the hair out of the way with a sectioning clip. ➔

2 To maximize the hair length and keep the braid of rolled hair close to the head, make two ponytails on top of each other behind the right ear. Secure with snag-free hair bands. ➔

3 Curl the ponytails in four or five sections each, using curling iron or a heated hair wand, as shown here. ➔

4 Unclip the front section and separate it vertically into three pieces. Secure each piece in place. Working with the section on the right first—closest to the ponytails—create a quiff by pulling the hair forward and backcombing toward the root. Smooth the hair back over toward the ponytails and grip the inside with bobby pins, placing them carefully so that they are not visible. ➡

5 Backcomb the middle section and smooth back toward the ponytail. Secure with a pin. Repeat this with the final section at the left of the head. ⬆

6 With a large bristle brush, smooth the loose ends of hair into the ponytails so that you have one long, curled roll that falls forward over the shoulder. ⬅

7 Secure a length of ribbon under the base of the top ponytail by forming an "X" with bobby pins. Wrap the ribbon around the hair, finishing about two inches from the bottom of the roll. Cut the ribbon. Use a bobby pin to hold the bottom end of the ribbon in place, pushing the grip up into the hair so that it is not visible. ↑

8 Tuck three or four white flowers behind the ribbon. Leaving a couple of inches of the stem intact will help to keep the flowers in place. ↩

PRO TIP

Artificial flowers are stiffer than natural ones and therefore easier to use and hold in place. They will also last longer.

Mayan girl

YOU WILL NEED

- ➔ Tail comb
- ➔ Hair bungees
- ➔ Bobby pins
- ➔ Hair bands
- ➔ Colored cord

1 Make a center part from the forehead all the way back to the neck using the point of a tail comb, thus dividing the hair into two. ➔

2 Secure the hair into two low pigtails on either side of the head using hair bands or snag-free bands. ⬅

3 One at a time, separate each pigtail in two and twist each section of hair. ➔

71

4 Wrap the twists around each other and tie the ends together using a band or a length of cord. ⬆

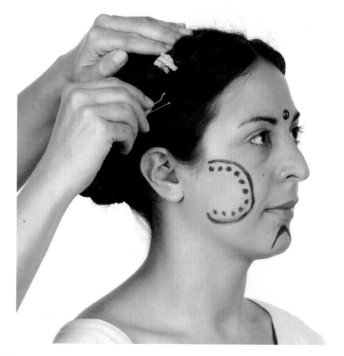

5 Secure each twist at the forehead by discreetly pinning with bobby pins, putting the pins in the rolls to conceal them. ➡

Eastern warrior

YOU WILL NEED

- Tail comb
- Bald cap
- Eyeliner pencil
- Tape
- Spirit gum
- Scissors
- Crepe hair
- Curling iron

1 Create a bald head using a bald cap. First, make sure that the model's own hair is gelled and combed flat. Clean the skin using a toner and make sure it is dry. ⬆

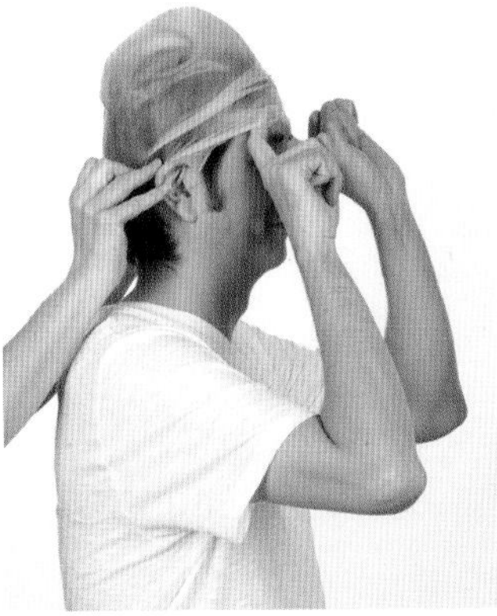

2 Ask the model to hold the front of the bald cap as you stretch it over from behind. It should sit just above the eyebrows. ⬆

3 Cut away the bulk of the extra cap at the front and tuck in any stray hairs. ⬇

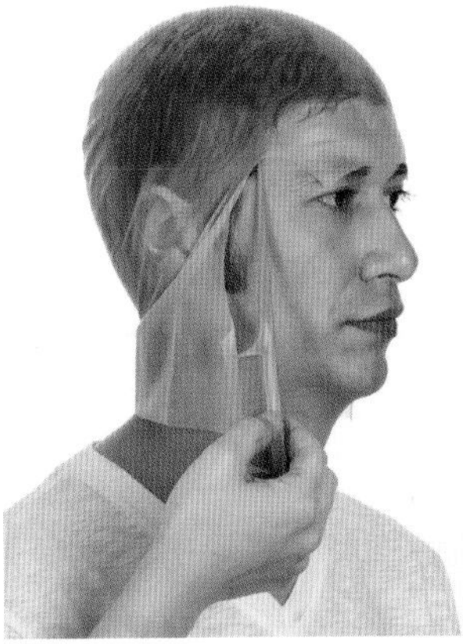

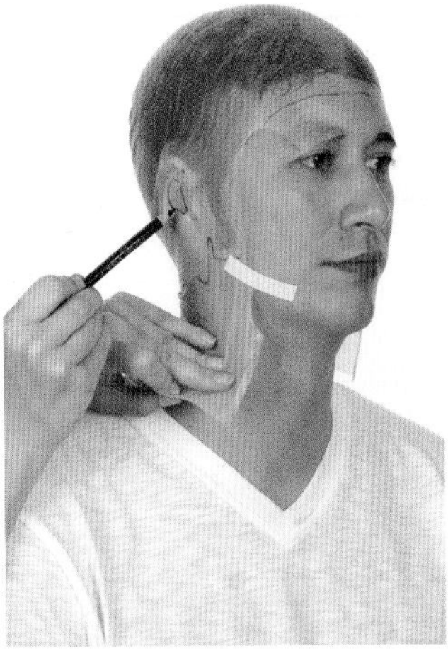

4 Tape the sides of the cap down to hold it in place. Draw a cutting line using an eyebrow pencil, drawing inside the ear and around the sideburns. ⬆

8 Use a base color all over the face and head. You will need a heavy cream base on the cap, such as a pan stick. ➜

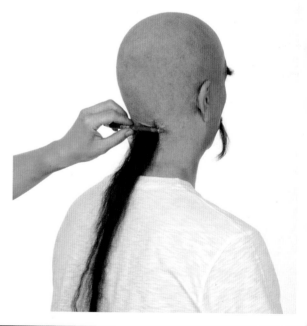

5 Cut away any extra cap using a pair of scissors. Carefully lift the edge along the front and glue it down using spirit gum. Firmly press down and hold with a velour puff. Remove the tape and glue down the side flaps. ⬆

6 Put some tape at the back of the neck, cut out inside the ear and tuck behind, gluing the cap down with spirit gum. ⬆

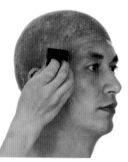

7 Color the cap, first applying a rosy red or pink color to counteract the color of the hair beneath the cap. Stipple the color on using a rubber stipple sponge. ⬆

9 Begin to lay the hair from the nape of the neck back toward the crown. Prepare long lengths of prepared crepe hair, the same color as the actor's eyebrows. Lay hair approximately two inches wide. Apply spirit gum to the bald cap then press hair onto it, firmly rolling with a pen or the handle of a brush. ⬇

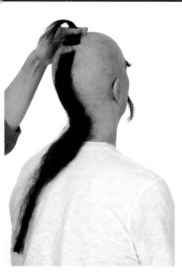

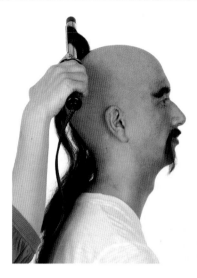

11 Wait for the spirit gum to dry. Create lift at the root of the hair on top by using the iron. ⮌

10 Work up toward the crown, laying the hair in rows. Once it has all been laid, lift the hair away from the head one row at a time from the crown down to the root. ⬆

PRO TIP

It is possible to make your own bald cap with latex, but much easier to buy a ready-made one.

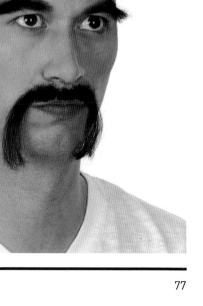

Celtic warrior

YOU WILL NEED

- ➔ Sectioning clips
- ➔ Tail comb
- ➔ Small-barreled curling iron
- ➔ Comb
- ➔ Crepe hair
- ➔ Styling spray
- ➔ Scissors

1 Section the hair into six sections and keep out of the way using sectioning clips. ➔

2 Using a small-barreled curling iron, take a section of hair at a time and create ringlets. ↩

3 Braid a length of crepe hair into the section of hair at each temple. The color of the crepe hair should match, as much as possible, the color of the model's own hair. ➔

5 Remove the sectioning clips from the rest of the hair and loosen the curls with your fingers. ⬆

4 Knot the end of the braid and cut to the desired length. ⬆

6 Tease the hair all over to give a disheveled look. ➡

7 Spray all over to set using hairspray. ↩

PRO TIP

The model's hair needs to be quite long for this look to work. Teasing wet, warm, or tangled hair increases the likelihood of tearing and damage, so make sure the hair has cooled properly before you begin teasing.

Italian Renaissance

YOU WILL NEED

- ➡ Sewn strip of real hair
- ➡ Hair bands
- ➡ Bobby pins
- ➡ Tail comb
- ➡ Hairspray

1 Take a length of real hair about 8in (20cm) wide and fold into a spiral. ➡

3 Divide the hair into three and braid. ⬇

2 Use a snag-free band to tie the hair just below the end, as you would tie the model's own hair against their head. ⬆

4 Tie at the end. Repeat steps 1–4 as many times as necessary, until you have the required number of braids for your look. ⬆

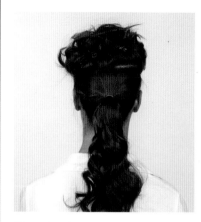

5 Section the model's hair horizontally into two, making a ponytail from the lower section of hair. ⬆

6 Divide the top section of hair into several smaller sections. ➡

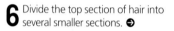

7 Just behind the top section of hair, pin the false braids above the crown of the head using bobby pins. ⬅

8 Section the lower portion of hair into two and create a bun, wrapping the sections over one another and pinning with bobby pins and anchoring with hair pins. ⬇

9 Unpin the hair just above the bun and backcomb lightly to create height and cover the ends of the braids. Tuck this hair neatly into the bun, wrapping the ends around the base of the bun, pinning to hold. ⬇

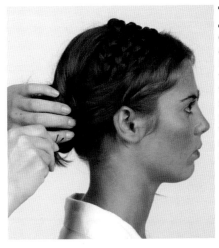

10 Unpin the front sections of hair and create a center part. Loosely pull back toward the bun and tuck the ends in, securing them with pins. Spray the bun well with hairspray and smooth down any stray hairs. ↩

PRO TIP

You can buy real hair loose, which is called a weft, or as a long length stitched onto a seam—this is easier to work with and manipulate. When adding hair to a bun in stages, remember the pins used to secure the first sections will be hidden by the hair you add later on. These pins can be quite big as they will create a good base to hook the finger pins into later.

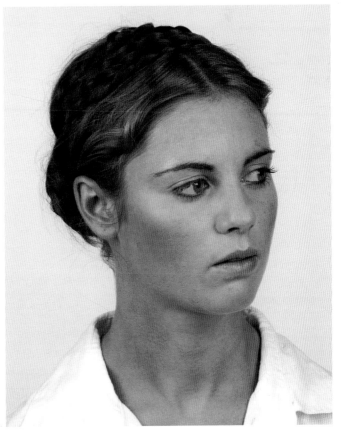

Elizabethan England

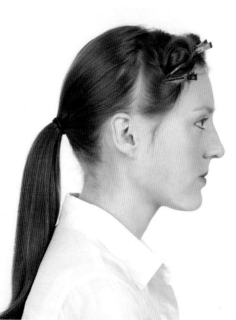

1 Separate the front and back of the hair using a tail comb to divide it from ear to ear. Separate the front section again in two (making three sections in total) on either side of the center part, and pull the back section into a smooth, low ponytail, securing with a bungee for a smoother finish. →

2 Putting the front sections of hair on large, heated rollers makes it easier to make the heart-shape rolls that characterize this hairstyle. Working back from the part, let the hair fall forward and roll the roller up toward the root. Hold the rollers in place with roller pins. →

3 Spray the smoothed ponytail and lightly backcomb it to make it easier to manipulate. Pull the hair through a bun ring. ↑

86

4 Spread the hair around the bun ring and pin at intervals all around to secure. Wrap the ends around and spray to tidy. If you find this hard to do, place a hair band over the bun ring to hold the ends, and then wrap the ends over the band to disguise it. ⊖

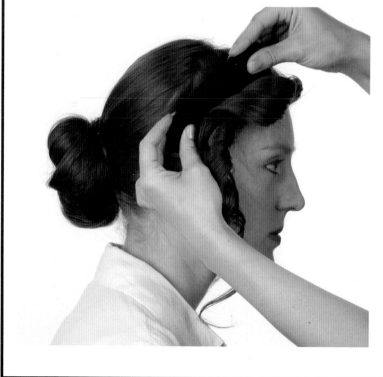

5 Remove the rollers and prepare a hair rat by cutting it to a suitable length (so it stretches from the part to just behind the ear), slightly shorter than the roll you are aiming to create. ⊖

6 Grip the hair rat in place with bobby pins. ⬇

7 Tease the hair, backcombing it lightly, and wrap it over the hair rat. Secure at intervals along the rat discreetly with hairpins. Tuck in the ends and secure with a bobby pin. ⬆

8 Spray to set. ➡

PRO TIP

A hair rat is a hair pad. You can buy them ready made, or you can make them by cutting up a bun ring or even collecting up the waste crepe hair used in other styles and stuffing it into a hair net and molding it into the desired shape.

Restoration

1 Create a center part using a tail comb. ➊

2 Section the hair into small sections for straightening. Hold in place by clipping with sectioning clips. ➌

4 Work the straighteners through the whole hair. Turn your wrists inward toward the actor's head, an inch from the ends, to create a soft curl at the bottom. ⬆

3 Straighten the hair, taking one section at a time, running the straighteners along the hair shaft, combing ahead of the straighteners as you go. ⬆

5 Spray to hold using hairspray. ➡

PRO TIP

When straightening hair, working on small sections of hair creates a smoother finish—perfect for this Restoration period look.

18th-century France (man)

YOU WILL NEED

- → Comb
- → Hairspray
- → Hair net
- → Wig
- → Colored hairspray
- → Tail comb
- → White aquapaint

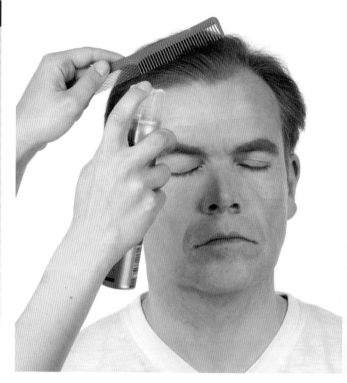

1 Comb hair away from the face. If required, gel the hair down and fix with hairspray. →

2 Place a hair net over the hair. ←

3 Ask the actor/model to hold the front of the wig firmly, close to their forehead. Pull the wig over the head. →

4 Using a tail comb, tuck any visible hairs and the hair net under the wig. ⬇

5 Dress the wig with a comb and spray into place. Color the wig with colored hairspray, using a tissue to protect the skin. ⬆

6 Color any of the actor's natural hair that is showing using white aquapaint to conceal smaller areas such as the sideburns. ⬅

PRO TIP

Good wigs are expensive and your budget will not always allow for the kind of wig that is on a lace and then glued to the forehead. This look is recreated using a cheaper wig, but the look can also be created using an expensive wig, or even using the actor's natural hair (see page 115).

18th-century France

1 Divide the hair into four horizontal sections and clip with sectioning clips. As you unclip a section to work on, spray it with styling tonic or mist with hairspray. ⬇

2 Use a medium-barreled curling iron to curl the hair, taking one section at a time. For a ringlet effect, wrap the hair around the iron vertically. ⬇

3 As you remove the hair from the iron, let it drop downward into ringlets. ⬅

4 Spray with hairspray
to set. ⏷

5 Separate the front hair around the forehead
from the rest of the hair and clip out of the
way. Take small sections of the hair around the
face and loosely pin to the crown. ⏷

6 Use the arm of the tail comb to
lift the pinned hair and create
a soft quiff that is higher in the
center. ⏷

7 Unclip the front, separate out a few wispy strands and pin the rest onto the crown. ⊙

8 Tease the wispy strands so that they sit just above the eyes. ⊙

PRO TIP

When curling the hair, hold the curling iron at the same angle as the curl you wish to create.

Regency England

YOU WILL NEED

- Sectioning clips
- Small-barreled curling iron
- Bun ring
- Hair bungee
- Hairspray
- Bobby pins
- Tail comb
- Sections of real hair sewn in a strip, to match model's own hair color

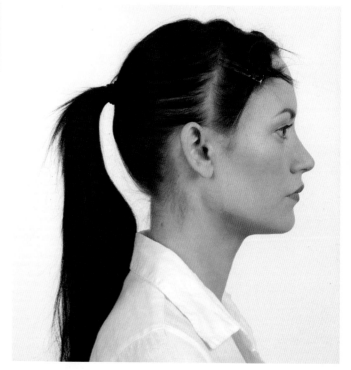

1 Make ringlets using a sewn strip of real hair (see page 24). ↑

2 Separate off the front section of hair from ear to ear and clip away. Pull the rest of the hair into a smooth ponytail, using a hair bungee to secure. ↑

3 Lightly spray the ponytail with hairspray and curl it with curling iron, taking small sections one at a time. ↩

4 Pull the hair through a bun ring and pin the ring into place. ◉

5 Take the hair one curl at a time and pin it over and around the bun ring. Keep the hand holding the hair loose as you grip each length so that you keep the ringlet shape intact. When all the hair is pinned, spray with hairspray. ◉

6 Using bobby pins, secure the false ringlets into the sides and base of the bun ring, placing four on either side. Trim the ringlets once they are in place if necessary, so that they are equal in length. ◉

7 Unpin the front sections and smooth them back into the pinned hair. Use this hair from the front of the head to cover any visible pins or ringlet seams and grip into place. If necessary, curl loose ends with the curling iron and pin them into the rest of the hair. ↰

8 Leave a few wisps of hair along the hairline free and curl them separately. ↴

PRO TIP

When curling hair, naturally letting the hair fall, with no brushing after, produces the kind of pristine, tight curls required for this look. When removing the curling iron from the hair, try to extract them so as to leave the curl in place, rather than unwinding the curls.

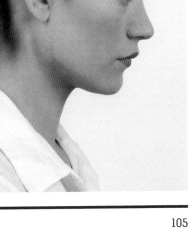

Imperial Russia

YOU WILL NEED

- ➔ Sectioning clips
- ➔ Ponytail brush
- ➔ Hair bungee
- ➔ Small-barreled curling iron
- ➔ Tail comb
- ➔ Hairspray

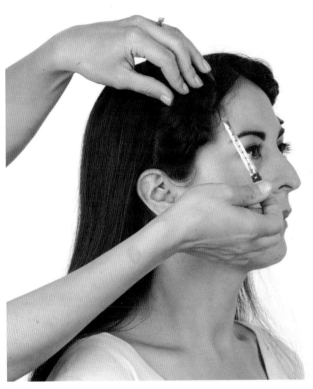

1 Divide the hair into front and back, sectioning across the head from one ear to the other using a tail comb, and clip the front section out of the way with a sectioning clip. ➔

2 Make a smooth, high ponytail using a ponytail brush. ➔

3 Secure with a hair bungee. ⬆

4 Conceal the hair bungee using a small section of the model's own hair. Wrap it around the bungee, gripping the end underneath with a bobby pin. ➔

5 Using a curling iron, curl the hair in the ponytail in small sections and spray with hairspray to hold. ⬆

6 Unclip the front section and divide into two along the center part. Comb with a fine tail comb to make it as smooth as possible. ➔

7 Comb down toward the nape of the neck under the ponytail and spray into place, pinning to secure the ends with bobby pins if necessary. ⊙

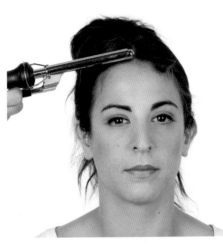

8 Make kiss curls around the forehead using a small barreled curling iron. Separate the curls with your fingers and spray to set. ⊖

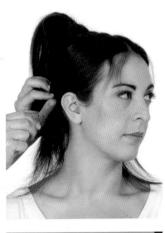

PRO TIP

If you find it hard to brush the hair smoothly up into the ponytail, ask the model to turn their head upside down. Use a hair bungee to secure (this gives a neater result than a band).

French aristocracy

YOU WILL NEED

- Ponytail brush
- Bun rings
- Tail comb
- Bobby pins
- Sections of real hair pieces, curled
- Hairspray
- Bow for decoration

1 Create a high ponytail using a ponytail brush and secure it with a hair bungee.

2 Place two bun rings at the base of the ponytail. Secure the bottom ring to the head using bobby pins. ➜

3 Smooth hair from the ponytail over the bun rings, using the tail of a tail comb, and pin the ends under the rings using hairpins. If the hair is very long, use a hair band to pull the ends in under the bun rings. ➡

4 Attach curls made from sewn sections of real hair (see page 24) to the bottom of the bun, securing each one with a bobby pin. ⬇

5 Pin the curls up around the bun, concealing any visible grips with the next section you pin. ⬆

6 Attach a curled ponytail-sized hairpiece to the back of the head, beneath the bun, and secure in place using grips. ⬆

8 Spray to set. ⬆

7 Add a bow to the front of the bun and pin in place. ⬆

PRO TIP

Make sure the additional sections of hairpiece are similar to the model's hair in texture, and identical in color. You may have to dye them so they match perfectly.

French Revolution

YOU WILL NEED

- Sectioning clips
- Curling iron
- Hair band
- Colored hairspray
- Ribbon
- Hairspray
- Bobby pins

1 Section the hair front and back from ear to ear, then divide the front section into three. ➜

3 Divide each section into two and clip one section out of the way. Use a small-barreled curling iron to curl the bottom section. ➜

2 Make a ponytail with the back section of hair and secure with a hair band. ➊

4 Pin the curl to the head and move up to the next section of hair. Curl and pin, repeating on the other side. ⬆

5 Lift sections of the top section of hair, starting at the front, and tease toward the root and spray. ⬇

6 Separate the hair around the hairline and sweep the remaining hair back toward the ponytail. Pin in place. ⬅

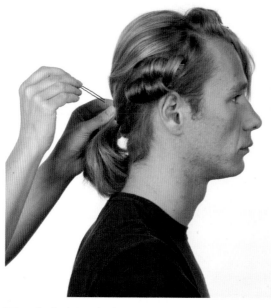

7 Unclip the hair at the front and use a tail comb to neatly comb over the teased hair. Spray with hairspray to hold and tidy the ends. ➡

8 Spray to hold in place and then whiten the hair with colored hairspray. ⊕

9 Finish by concealing the hair band by tying a black ribbon over the top, finished in a bow. ⊕

PRO TIP

When using colored hairspray, use a tissue to protect the model's eyes, and to act as a stencil to protect the model's makeup.

Pirate

YOU WILL NEED

- ➔ Curling iron
- ➔ Tail comb
- ➔ Sectioning clips
- ➔ String and beads
- ➔ Cloth headband

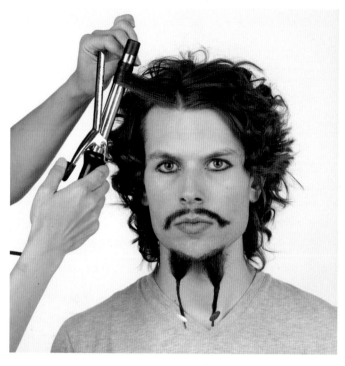

1 Use a curling iron all over the hair to create volume and a shaggy look. ➔

2 Roughly loosen sections of the hair with your fingers, brushing them away from the face. ➔

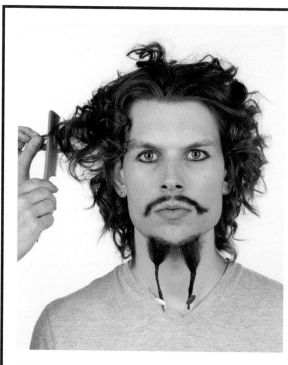

4 Pick out a small section of hair and clip the rest of the hair out of the way with sectioning clips. Divide into three equal parts and braid the hair. ◑

3 Using a tail comb, backcomb the ends of small sections of hair all over the head. ◑

5 Tie the end of the braid using string and dress with decorative beads. Repeat the braiding process a few times with random sections of hair. ➡

6 Unpin the hair and dress the hair with a cloth headband. ☞

PRO TIP

This look needs to be done on a model or actor with quite long hair, otherwise you will need to attach sewn sections of hair to add length for the braids. Use unwashed hair for easier styling.

Wild-west girl

1 Split the hair in half down the center of the head using a tail comb. Loosely secure each section. ➊

2 Smooth the sections one at a time into low pigtails, which should sit behind the ear on the hairline. Secure each pigtail with a snag-free hairband. ➋

3 Take a small section of hair from the underside of one of the pigtails and wrap it round the hair band to conceal the band. Secure the end of this concealing section with a small bobby pin. Place the grip under the pigtail so it is not visible. ➊

123

4 Repeat on the other side. ⊘

5 Curl the bottom half of each pigtail into loose ringlets using a curling wand or iron. ⊜

6 Brush out the curls in each pigtail. Spray with hairspray and repeat on the other side. ➡

PRO TIP

The part for this look does not need to be too perfect—it is quite a natural look so keep the curls gentle and the hair not overly sprayed.

Napoleonic

YOU WILL NEED

- Water
- Four braids made from hair pieces (see page 22)
- Hairspray
- Tail comb
- Sectioning clips
- Bobby pins

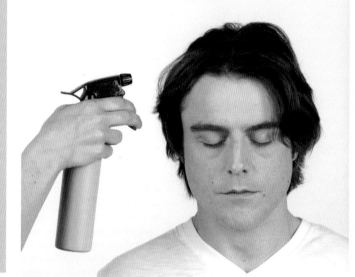

1 Lightly spritz the model's hair all over with water. ⊙

2 Using a tail comb, work the model's hair into the final desired shape, creating a side part. ⊙

3 Use your hands to mold and create volume on the sides. Spray with hairspray to fix. ⊙

4 Two braids should be placed on either side of the head, using the tail of the tail comb to lift the hair above where you want the root of the braid to go—clip this out of the way. ⬆

5 Tease the hair lightly to create a base for pinning the braid. Use bobby pins to secure the braid to the head. ⬇

6 Remove the hair from the clips and smooth down over the top of the braid to conceal the grips and root of the braid. ⬆

PRO TIP

When attaching the hair braids, for stability, make an "X" with the grips by crossing the second over the top of the first.

Victorian gentleman

YOU WILL NEED

- ● Tail comb
- ● Styling gel
- ● Sectioning clips
- ● Hairdryer
- ● White aquapaint

1 Work hair gel through the hair with your fingers. ●

2 Using a tail comb, create a deep side part. ●

3 To set the hair, pin it in place. ⬆

4 Dry the gel into the hair and set the style by blasting with a hairdryer. ⬆

5 Paint white aquapaint along the part line to emphasize it. Remove the clips and spray with hairspray to hold the style. ↩

PRO TIP

This look is very clean, unlike earlier looks
from the period that were bushier and
oiled, rather than gelled. For best results,
your model should have hair about 2in
(5cm) long.

Victorian matriarch

YOU WILL NEED

- Medium heated rollers
- Hairspray
- Sectioning clip
- Brush
- Hairpins
- Tail comb

1 Separate the hair at the crown into two sections, front and back, then split the front section into two down the center part. Set all the hair on medium-sized heated rollers. ⊕

3 Brush through back section to smooth, roll into chignon and secure with hairpins, leaving ends loose. ⊜

2 Remove rollers one section at a time and loosen hair with fingers. Spray with hairspray to create friction, gather hair at the ends and clip with sectioning clips to keep in sections. ⊕

135

4 Take one of the front sections and backcomb the ends to create volume (don't backcomb the roots). ⬆

5 Collect all of the hair in this section into the palm of your hand, lift toward the crown and roll inward. ⬆

6 With the thin end of the tail comb, draw hair outward from the roots to create a puff. Secure with hairpins, and tuck in the ends. ⬆

7 Repeat on the other side, smooth down any loose ends and spray with hairspray to fix. ⊖

8 Backcomb loose ends from the chignon, smooth into curls and pin neatly into the top of the chignon. ⊕

PRO TIP

Instead of creating a chignon at the back, try carrying the roll around the head, tucking in all the ends neatly to create a more severe look.

Upper-class Victorian lady

YOU WILL NEED

- ➲ Styling lotion
- ➲ Rollers or perming rods
- ➲ Hair band
- ➲ Hairspray
- ➲ Sectioning clips
- ➲ Drying hood
- ➲ Hairdryer
- ➲ Hair pad or rat
- ➲ Bobby pins
- ➲ Tail comb

1 Spritz the hair with styling lotion and comb to create a center part. ⬆

2 With the smallest roller or perming rod available, begin to set the hair on rollers from the front, curling tightly and working backward. The hair should come forward at either side of the part. Take thick sections the same width as the roller, and work down each side of the part from the top toward the ears. ➲

3 Section the hair at the back of the head, working down from the crown toward the nape of the neck. These sections should be thicker, using larger rollers and sectioning hair so that each section is the same width as the roller that is being used. Curl the hair until you reach halfway down the back of the head and put the rest of the hair into a ponytail. Spray all over. ⬆

5 Clip the curls on top and at the sides using sectioning clips to make sure they stay in place while you work on the back. ⊙

4 Set by sitting the model under a drying hood for 15 minutes. Remove the curlers from the hair, unwinding them slowly but not loosening the curl. ⊙

6 Uncurl a few curls at the back and backcomb. Gather the hair together and secure the hair pad behind this section of hair using bobby pins. ⊙

7 Tease the hair back over the hair pad, backcombing where necessary, and pin in place. To build up curls over the hair pad, adding height and volume, separate each curl out, tease it and pin in place. Pin the curls at the sides of the head. ⊙

8 Backcomb and tease the ponytail, twisting and winding it into a small, neat bun and pinning it into place with hairpins. ⟱

9 Remove the sectioning clips carefully. Keeping each roll in its coiled shape, pull the end of each roll back toward the pinned bit of hair (like stretching out a spring) and secure it inside the roll to the body of hair with a bobby pin. Tidy any stray hairs and spray. ⟱

PRO TIP

Sit the model in front of a mirror so you can keep an eye on what the front looks like as you're pinning the curls into place.

Poor Victorian

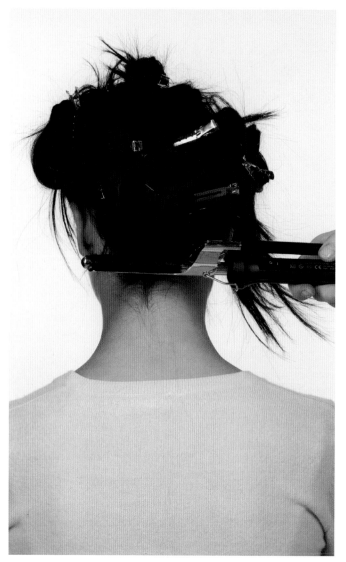

2 Spray the hair with hairspray to fix. ⬇

1 Section the hair with sectioning clips. Starting at the nape of the neck, curl the hair with a small-barreled curling iron. If the model has very thick hair, not all of it needs to be curled—the bulk of it can be pinned to the head. ⬆

3 Pull the curled lengths away from the model's head one by one. Backcomb each length lightly, working from the ends of the hair toward the root. Backcombing will add volume and create a messy look. ⮐ + ⮑

4 Tuck the bulk of the hair onto the head and pin it to the crown with bobby pins. ➜

PRO TIP

Unwashed hair is better for styling— work from dry and spritz with water and styling spray.

5 Shake stage dirt or charcoal powder over the head to dirty it. Loosen the sides to add a straggly look framing the cheeks. ⊙

US Civil War soldier

YOU WILL NEED

- ➔ Crepe hair
- ➔ Pen
- ➔ Scissors
- ➔ Spirit gum
- ➔ Tail comb

1 Lay a mustache using prepared crepe hair, working along the top lip starting in the middle and working outward. ➔

2 Apply spirit gum to the skin and wait for it to go tacky. Gather a small bunch of crepe hair, push the tips into the glue and firmly press it in with a pen, using an outward rolling motion. ➔

3 Build the hair up in layers along the lip first and then working upward toward the nose. Use different shades of hair—darker on the base and becoming blonder on top and trim to a length just above the top lip. ➔

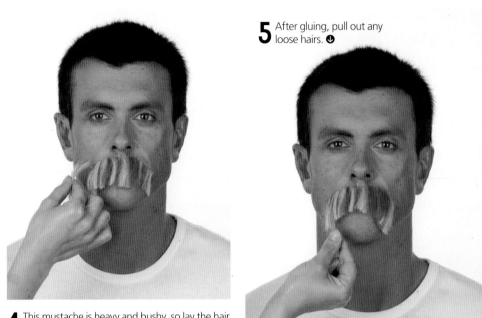

5 After gluing, pull out any loose hairs. ⬇

4 This mustache is heavy and bushy, so lay the hair thickly and leave it long enough so it hangs over the lips. ⬆

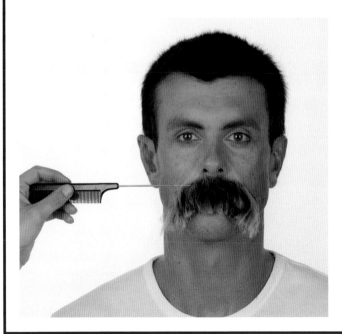

6 Lift between the hairs with a tail comb to separate them and cut a line along the bottom of the mustache. Then cut into it vertically for a more natural look. ➡

PRO TIP

The mustache has its own ply. Depending on the shape, start laying it at the sides for a wispy mustache, or in the middle and apply in layers for a thicker mustache.

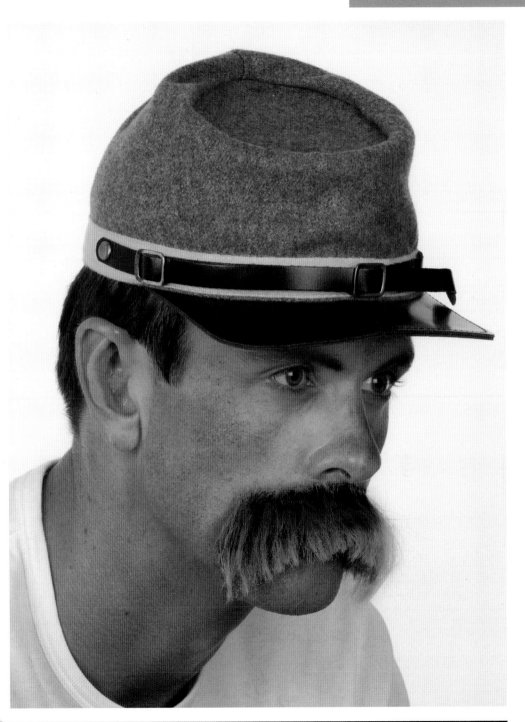

US Civil War lady

YOU WILL NEED

- Sectioning clips
- Hair straighteners
- Tail comb
- Long bobby pins
- Hair net
- Hair bungee
- Hairpins

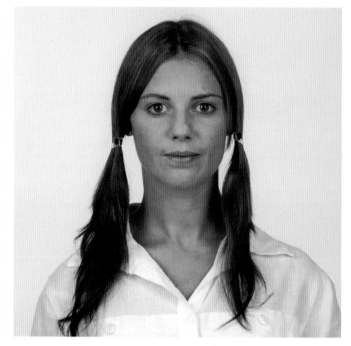

1 Divide the front section in two using a tail comb to create a very straight center part. ⬆

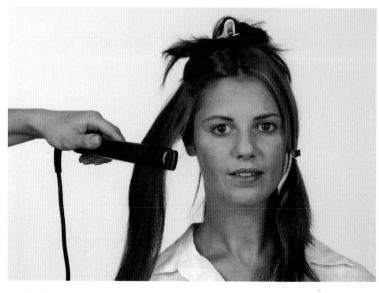

2 Using hair straighteners, smooth through the hair. ➡

3 Create a roll on either side of the head by holding the hair near the bottom in one hand while scissoring the hair between index and middle fingers with the other hand. Lift the bottom hand, taking the hair under and backward. ⊙

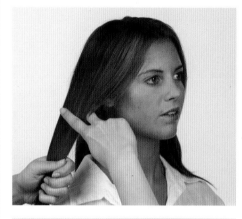

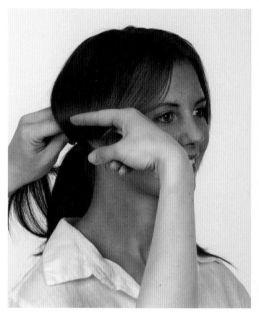

4 Hold the hair in place by inserting the index finger of your rear hand into the roll you have created. ⊙

5 Release the front hand and use it to secure the hair with a long bobby pin, placing the pin into the roll from the back toward the front. Repeat this rolling and gripping on the other side of the head. ⊙

6 Gather all the hair together in a ponytail and secure with a hair bungee. ⊙

7 Lightly backcomb the hair to create friction and volume. ↑

8 Lift the ponytail up and place a hair net underneath, securing it with a bobby pin. ↑

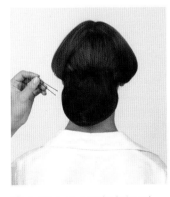

9 Pull the net over the hair and secure again with hairpins. ↑

PRO TIP

Teasing hair is an essential skill. It's also known as "backcombing" because it involves combing or brushing back toward the root to create small tangles that will make the hair easier to mold. When done properly, it will add substance to any hairstyle.

Native American

YOU WILL NEED

- → Bald cap
- → Crepe hair
- → Glue
- → Hair straighteners
- → Scissors
- → Gel
- → Hairspray

1 Apply a bald cap (see page 75). ↷

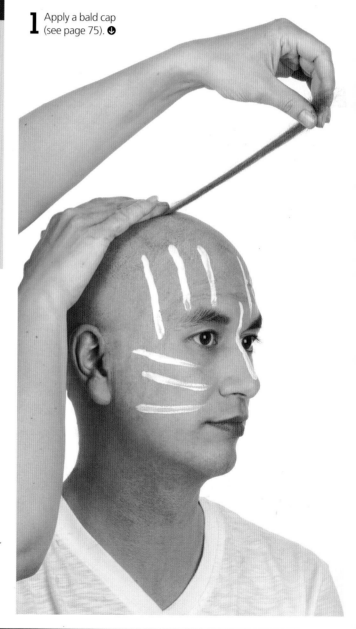

2 Begin creating your Mohican by laying crepe hair small sections at a time, starting at the crown two inches back from the hairline, and gluing it at a 45-degree angle in the center. ↑

5 Starting at the back of the head, run straighteners through the hair. ➡

3 Lay the hair forward in layers, a section at a time, applying glue to the bald cap rather than the hair itself. After you lay each section, press it firmly with a pen or velour puff and hold down until the glue dries. ⬆

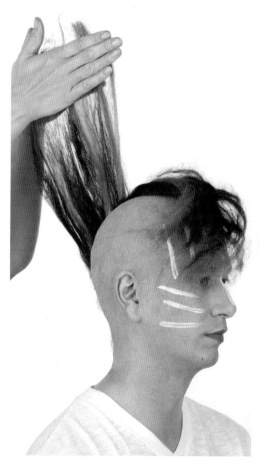

4 Once the glue is dry, apply hair gel. ⬆

6 Smooth extra-strength hair gel through the length of the hair. ⬆

7 Trim the ends and spray. Dry vigorously with a hairdryer for extra hold. ⊙

PRO TIP

You'll need strong hair gel to hold the hair in place for this look. Try straightening after applying gel as well as before, to set the style in place.

YOU WILL NEED

- ➔ Sectioning clips
- ➔ Hair bungee
- ➔ Tail comb
- ➔ Bobby pins
- ➔ Hairspray

Geisha

1 Section the hair into two from ear to ear and divide the front section into two again. ⬆

2 Using a hair bungee, make a high ponytail from the main bulk of the hair and secure it at the back of the head. ⬆

3 Fold the hair in the ponytail over and then, using bobby pins, attach the ponytail to the head in a large, smooth roll. ⟲

5 Taking one section at a time, gently backcomb each section and fold backward, creating a roll. ⬇

4 Unpin the front sections of hair and divide into three equal sections, front, middle and two sides. ⬆

6 Secure the rolls at the front to the head by inserting a bobby pin into the middle of the roll and either tuck the ends in or tidy them into the rest of the hair. Spray to set and add a spray of flowers or decorate with a brooch. ⬅

PRO TIP

Straighten and smooth curly hair before you attempt to recreate this look.

YOU WILL NEED

- Tail comb
- Heated rollers
- Clips
- Bobby pins
- Hair band
- Roller pins

Edwardian

1 Section the hair into layers, beginning at the crown of the head, and clip. ⬆

2 Put the hair into large, heated rollers and hold in place with roller pins. Work around the head, starting at the back from the nape of the neck and finishing on the crown. ⬆

3 Leave the rollers for fifteen minutes to cool. ↩

4 Unroll the rollers, starting at the crown. ⬇

5 Tidy the hair on the crown into a small bun—twist the hair and roll it in a circle onto the head, securing with pins. ⬇

6 Remove the rollers one at a time from the neck upward, leaving the top front rollers in place. Pin each curl loosely to the bun as you go. ⬇

7 When you get to the sides, unroll and tease lightly. Create a roll back away from the face using your hand as a guide, and grip inside the roll so the bobby pin is hidden. ⬆

8 Unroll the rollers on top, and pin in place using bobby pins. ⊙

9 Tease and pin the front curls in place so they frame the face. ⊙

PRO TIP

To tease the hair, lightly brush toward the scalp while continuing to hold up the strand firmly with your other hand. Hold each curl in position while you are pinning it to the head by placing the tail of a tail comb inside the curl as you pin. This will help to keep the structure of the curl while you pin.

America's sweetheart

YOU WILL NEED

- ➔ Sectioning clips
- ➔ Curling iron
- ➔ Hairbrush
- ➔ Bobby pins
- ➔ Styling spray
- ➔ String of pearls

1 Separate off a section of hair on top of the head between the ear and the crown, coming forward, and clip with a sectioning clip. ➔

2 To create big, loose curls with a medium-sized barrel curling iron/conical wand, take one section at a time, working from the nape of the neck upward and round to the sides. Spray hair. ➔

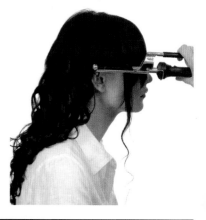

3 With a smaller barrel curling iron, curl the front section of hair. ➔

4 Tease out the curls from the back section to create chunky, loose ringlets with a soft bristle brush, backcombing for volume. ➡

5 Sweep the front section forward across to the other ear, rolling the ends under the side between the middle and index finger and securing in place with a bobby pin. ⬇

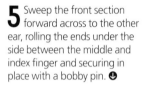

6 Drape pearls around the head and secure with a bobby pin. Make a cross with two bobby pins to anchor the pearls. Take the pearls around the front of the head and pin at the back. Circle the pearls around the head, securing with a bobby pin each time at the back. Spray to set. ⬆

PRO TIP

Curl the hair starting at the root, curling upward and working toward the ends for a more natural curl and for root lift.

Jazz-age flapper

YOU WILL NEED

- Sectioning clips
- Heated rollers
- Bobby pins
- Hair band
- Styling spray
- Hair bungee

1 Make a center part and set hair onto heated rollers on either side of it. Place a circle of big rollers at the very top of the head, a circle of medium rollers just outside, and a circle of small rollers outside that. ➔

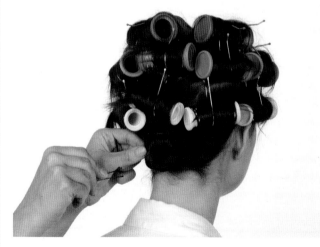

2 Take the hair in the middle of the back of the head out of the way. Tie it in a low ponytail, wrap the hair in the ponytail up into a small bun, and secure with bobby pins. Wait 15 minutes for the rollers to cool. ➔

3 Unroll the rollers, starting with the lower ones at the back before moving upward. Tuck the hair under and pin the curls into place as you unroll, using long bobby pins so you can insert the pin right into the barrel of the curl. Backcomb the roots before pinning. Work right round the head, unrolling a single layer of rollers. ⬆

4 Move onto the next layer of rollers, smoothing the hair over the layer below and pinning underneath to create a bob. Fold the roll of hair under the first row of rolls that you have made. ⬆

5 Move onto the top layer of rolls. Backcomb the roots for fullness as you remove the rollers. Dress the hair into place. Spray to fix. ⬅

PRO TIP

The bob was the style of the Jazz Age—this look is recreated using a model with longer hair.

1930s depression

YOU WILL NEED

- Styling spray
- Tail comb
- Sectioning clips
- Small-barreled curling iron (optional)
- Wax or pomade

1 Spritz thoroughly all over with styling spray. ➡

2 Make a side part using the point of a tail comb. ⬆

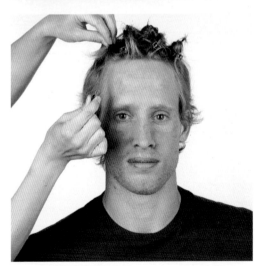

3 Clip hair into sections horizontally across the head. ⬅

4 If you want a wavy look and the actor or model has straight hair, use a small-barreled curling iron to create the waves. ➲

5 When the hair has been ironed all over, loosen the curls with your fingers and work into the desired shape. ⬅

6 Hold the style with wax or, for a more worn or greasy look, use hair pomade. ➲

PRO TIP

If adding waves to the hair, start at
the lowest point and work upward
(this may be the nape of the neck
or above the ear, depending on the
actor's hair length).

1930s Hollywood starlet

YOU WILL NEED

- ➲ Styling lotion
- ➲ Sectioning clips
- ➲ Heated rollers
- ➲ Small-barreled curling iron
- ➲ Pins
- ➲ Bobby pins
- ➲ Tail comb
- ➲ Hairspray

1 Divide the hair into sections that reflect the desired finished shape. Create a deep part, leaving the hair around the hairline unparted, and spritz with styling lotion. ⬆

2 Set the sides on small heated rollers. Sweep the top section to one side and set the ends onto a roller. Make small pin curls along the front hairline. Hold in place with bobby pins and curl in the desired final direction. ➡

3 Once they are cooled, remove the rollers and gently loosen the curls with your fingers. ↶

4 Tuck the ends under the body of the curls and pin with bobby pins so the hair sits above the shoulders. Spray with hairspray to fix. →

5 Unpin the pin curls and dress into place. Spray all over with hairspray to fix. ↓

PRO TIP

It is much easier to recreate this look on a model whose hair is too long, rather than too short, as the hair can easily be tucked under and this will also add volume.

1930s leading man

YOU WILL NEED

- ➔ Comb
- ➔ Small, narrow straighteners
- ➔ Pomade
- ➔ Hairspray

1 Comb the hair into the desired shape, lifting from the root for lots of volume. ⬆

2 Using small, narrow straigheners, lift the hair from underneath and curl it forward as you get to the ends of the hair. Reverse the direction of your wrist and flick away. ➔

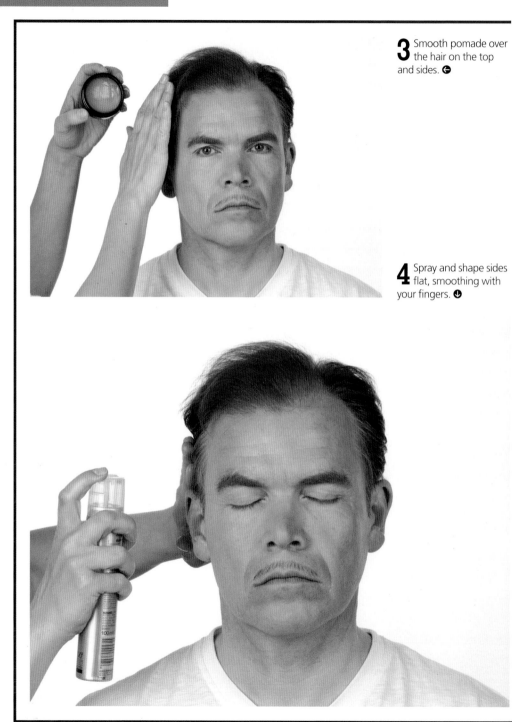

3 Smooth pomade over the hair on the top and sides. ⬅

4 Spray and shape sides flat, smoothing with your fingers. ⬇

PRO TIP

Use pomade sparingly—it's much easier to add more than to take away.

WWII forces' sweetheart

YOU WILL NEED

- Hair bungee
- Bobby pins
- Bun ring
- Clear, snag-free hair band
- Hairspray
- Ponytail brush
- Tail comb

1 Prepare bun ring with extra hair (see page 23). ↑

2 Smooth the model's hair into a very high ponytail (see page 20) and secure with a band or bungee. ↩

3 Fold the ends of the ponytail forward over the bun ring and roll it down toward the head, creating a horseshoe shape as you reach the scalp. Grip with pins. →

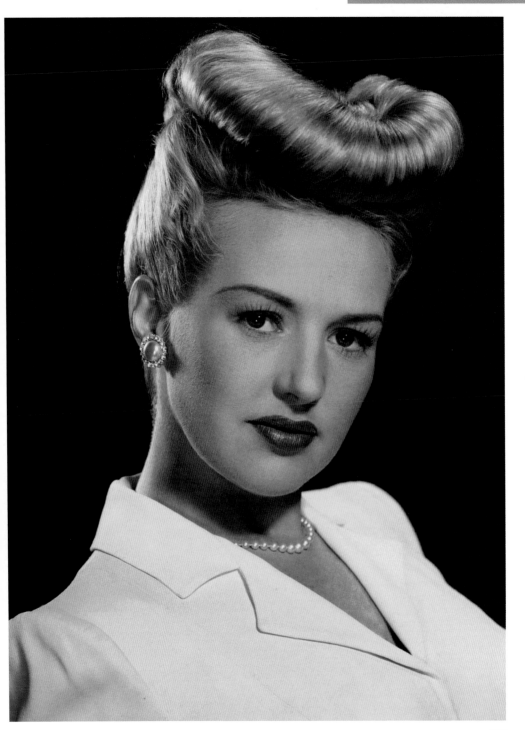

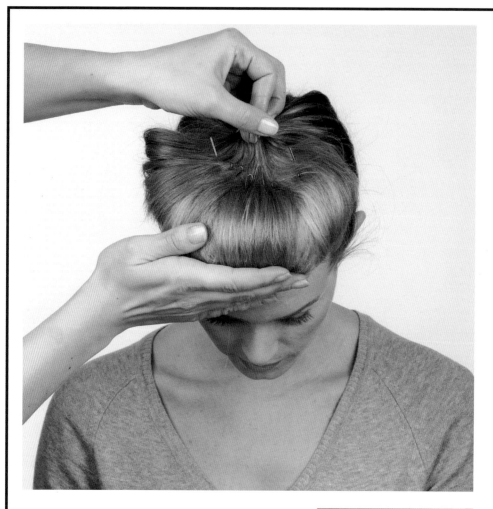

4 Push down the large mushroom shape in the center of the head and grip it flat against the scalp. Spray with hairspray to fix. ↑

PRO TIP

When creating this look, it is useful to have an extra pair of hands available to help you. Using a ponytail also makes it easier to achieve tightness.

WWII soldier

YOU WILL NEED

- ➔ Wet-look hair gel
- ➔ Fine tail comb
- ➔ Sectioning clips
- ➔ Hairdryer
- ➔ White aquacolor
- ➔ Hairspray

1 Work wet-look gel through the hair. ➊

2 Comb the hair with a fine tail comb and divide into a side part. ➊

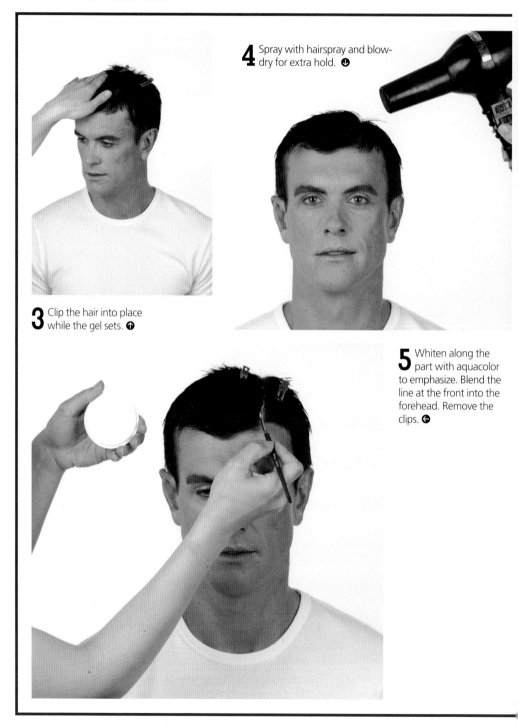

3 Clip the hair into place while the gel sets. ⬆

4 Spray with hairspray and blow-dry for extra hold. ⬇

5 Whiten along the part with aquacolor to emphasize. Blend the line at the front into the forehead. Remove the clips. ⬅

PRO TIP

This is a very slick, clean look that, because of the hair length, works better with gel than pomade.

1940s glamour

YOU WILL NEED

- Clear, snag-free hair bands
- Tail comb
- Long bobby pins
- Sectioning clips
- Small-barreled curling iron
- Hairspray

1 Divide the hair into sections that reflect the desired shape. ⬆

2 Using a small-barreled curling iron, create tight corkscrew curls all over the head, starting from the bottom and working upward. ⬆

3 When curling the front section, curl it backward, away from the forehead. ⬅

6 Spray all over with hairspray to fix. ⬆

7 Taking sections of the curls, tuck and pin them around the middle of the head, making the three ponytails appear as one piece with no gaps. ⬇

4 Make three ponytails down the center of the head. Secure with a hair band, leaving the front section separate. ⬆

5 Lightly backcomb the hair in the ponytails, starting at the top. ⬆

8 Unpin the front and dress into the required
style, securing with pins where necessary.
Spray liberally with hairspray. ⊙

PRO TIP

Pin curls are the authentic
1930s and 1940s setting
technique; however, they
do take some dexterity
and practice to master. A
curling iron is the modern
alternative and is quicker
and easier to use.

YOU WILL NEED

- Water
- Comb
- Hair bungee
- Gel
- Hairspray
- Hairdryer

Gangster chic

1 Wet hair thoroughly by spritzing with water. ⬆

3 If the actor or model's hair is longer than required for the look, secure the extra length in a low ponytail at the nape of the neck. ⬅

2 Comb hair with a wide-tooth comb in the direction of the final desired shape. ⬆

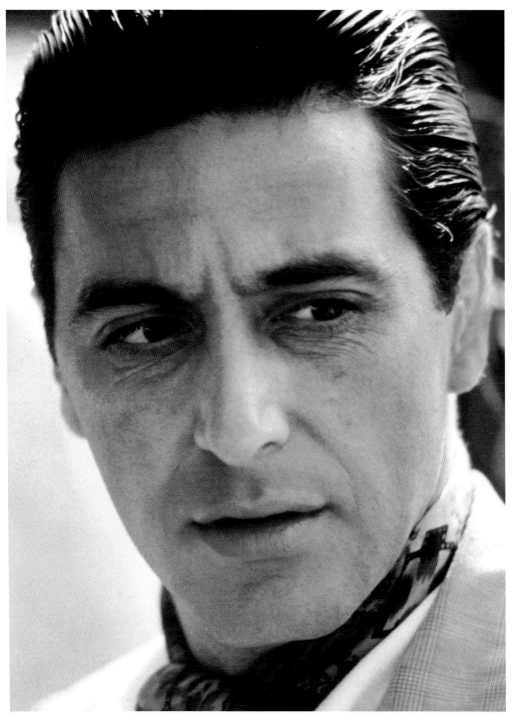

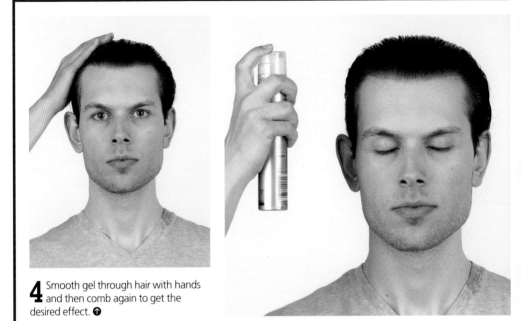

4 Smooth gel through hair with hands and then comb again to get the desired effect. ⊕

5 Spray with hairspray to hold in place and to ensure the gel retains a wet look. ⊕

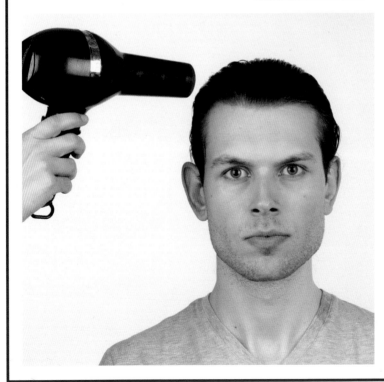

6 To firmly set, dry with a hairdryer on a medium setting. ⊕

PRO TIP

This look is flawless—don't hold back with the gel or hairspray as a wet look is desired and the hair should set so that it doesn't move out of place.

Blonde bombshell

YOU WILL NEED

- ➔ Styling lotion
- ➔ Heated rollers
- ➔ Hairspray
- ➔ Tail comb
- ➔ Sectioning clips

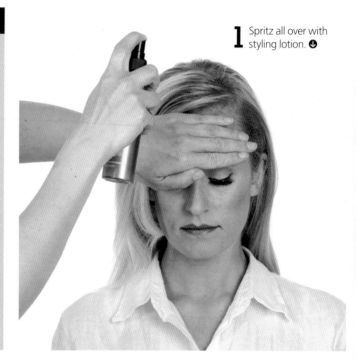

1 Spritz all over with styling lotion. ⬇

2 Set hair on heated rollers. Starting on top at the front, create a side part and use the set of the rollers to complement the shape of the final desired style. The size of each section of hair should be similar to the width of the roller. Use small- to medium-sized heated rollers and roller pins. The rollers should be smaller around the front of the head and medium on top. ➔

3 Spray with hairspray and leave the rollers to go cold. ⬆

4 As you remove each roller, lift the curls vertically and tease the roots, backcombing lightly for volume and root lift. Spray to hold. ⬆

6 Mold the hair into the desired shape with your hands, and spray vigorously. ⬆

5 Section off the front hair and tease the curls to make them easier to mold, as well as making long hair appear shorter to match the style of the times. ⬆

7 Unclip the top section of the hair, lift from the root with your fingers, and dress into place. ⬆

PRO TIP

Remove rollers by sliding curls out rather than unwinding, so that they keep their shape.

YOU WILL NEED

- Styling tonic
- Sectioning clips
- Small-barreled curling iron
- Bobby pins
- Hairspray

1950s flip

1 Spritz dry hair all over with styling tonic and divide into sections for blow-drying.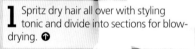

2 Blow-dry hair, starting at the neck and working upward. Create volume and lift from the root with a large-barreled, round brush. When you reach the ends, reverse the brush and roll outward to create a flick.

3 Divide the hair vertically into two sections, separating the top section from the rest of the hair about two inches above the ears. Divide this top section into three. Working on the back section first, backcomb from tip to root, and spray to create hold and friction.

4 Smooth the front of the section and let it drop backward to meet the rest of the hair. Push it back up gently to create shape, and smooth down on top. Spray to secure and repeat on the side sections. ➡

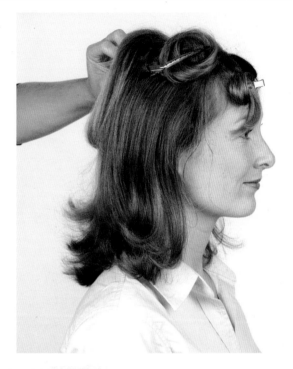

5 Curl the ends with a small-barreled curling iron. Roll the iron through two turns, moving around the head until all the ends are curled. ⬅

6 Brush through the curled ends with a comb to loosen the curls and combine all the way around the head. Fix with hairspray from underneath so the style keeps its shape. ⬆

7 Sweep front section over forehead and secure with bobby pins. Spray all over with shine spray and smooth down loose hairs. ⬆

PRO TIP

Use straighteners to create the flicks by rolling your wrist upward as you reach the ends of the hair.

YOU WILL NEED

- ➔ Sectioning clips
- ➔ Tail comb
- ➔ Bobby pins

1950s housewife

1 Section off a small area of hair near the forehead. ⬆

2 Backcomb the hair gently with a tail comb to add volume to it. ⬆

3 Sweep half of the unsectioned hair across from one side to the other, and make a seam of bobby pins up the head from the nape of the neck toward the crown, slightly off-center. ⬅

4 Gather all the hair together and roll it around your hand. Press the roll into the head and secure it in place with bobby pins. Using your other hand, push bobby pins vertically down into the roll to form a line. ⬇

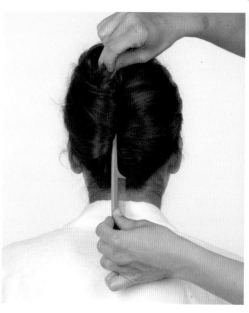

5 Tuck the ends of the twisted hair into the roll using the tail end of a tail comb, and pin along the seam discreetly with hairpins. ⬆

6 Unpin the section of hair at the front of the head and divide it in two. Backcomb the rear section lightly toward the root and spray. ⬇

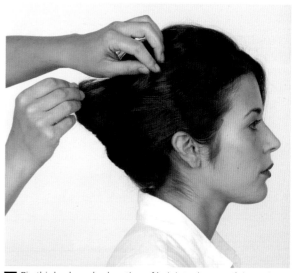

7 Pin this backcombed section of hair into the top of the twist, keeping it full. ⬆

8 Dress the front section of remaining hair, lifting it vertically at the root and teasing for height. ⬇

9 Take the hair to one side and tuck behind the ear using a grip to secure. ↩

PRO TIP

This look works best with pre-existing bangs, but if your model doesn't have any you can always tuck the hair under and pin the ends inside to give the illusion of bangs.

1950s glamour

YOU WILL NEED

- ➔ Tail comb
- ➔ Rollers
- ➔ Bobby pins
- ➔ Hairspray

2 Lightly backcomb the ends of the hair all over; this will make it easier to pin. Use a tail comb and begin backcombing for height at the root of the hair on the crown. Push the hair toward the root with small strokes of the comb. Clip the hair on the crown out of the way. ⬇

1 Use rollers to obtain the correct bang shape. Hold a roller at the ends of the hair and roll it down toward the root, tucking in the ends with a tail comb as you go. ⬆

3 Smooth the right-hand side of the hair with a brush, brushing toward the left side of the head. Spray to fix. Make a line of bobby pins slightly to the right of center, vertically up the back of the head. ⬅

5 Unclip the top section of the hair. Smooth it over and tease into shape with a tail comb. Secure the shape with pins, tucking the ends into the top of the chignon. ⬇

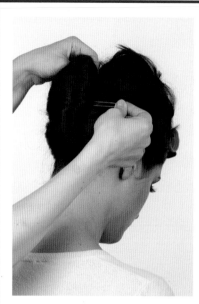

4 Fold the hair across your hand from left to right, rolling it around your hand as you fold. Holding the hair in position with your left hand, place a couple of long bobby pins into the centre of the roll, and place pins along the seam with your right hand to secure. ⬆

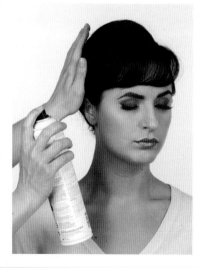

6 Unroll the bangs and dress into shape, pinning with bobby pins if necessary. Spray vigorously to set. ↩

PRO TIP

This look works best with straight hair. It also requires a lot of volume so it is worth taking extra time to backcomb the hair thoroughly before you start to style.

YOU WILL NEED

- Styling spray
- Hair mousse
- Sectioning clips
- Hairdryer
- Large, round hairbrush
- Hairspray

Rock 'n' roll

1 Spray hair all over with styling spray. ⊙

2 Work mousse into the hair. ⊙

3 Section the hair for blow-drying. ⊙

4 Blow-dry hair, starting at the sides. Use a small round brush, rolling the wrist outward. ⬇

5 Unpin the top section of hair and dry backward, working away from the face at a 45-degree angle for extra volume and lift. ⬆

6 Mold with hands, and spray with hairspray to set. ⬇

PRO TIP

Start with damp, towel-dried hair. For curly hair use more product, to avoid the end result having any frizz to it. Naturally straight hair is less likely to frizz.

1960s chick

1 Section the top of the hair into bangs, top middle, sides and crown. ⊙

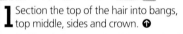

2 Make a hair pad with crepe hair and a hair net, or use an opened bun ring (see page 23). ⊖

3 Use a curling iron to create a curl on the ends of the hair. Comb through the curled ends and tuck them around the hair pad, rolling the pad toward the neck. ⊙

4 The roll of hair will be longer than the pad but the pad will give stability and keep the size of the roll uniform. Secure the roll in place by inserting bobby pins into either end of it, and pin along the seam with hairpins. ⬇

5 Unclip the top, middle section and backcomb the hair at the root from behind. Spray and let it fall forward. ⬅

6 Using bobby pins, grip a pad made of crepe hair behind the hair, to create the base of a beehive. ⬇

7 Smooth the backcombed hair over the pad using a tail comb. Bunch the hair together and pin it in place. ⬆

8 Unclip the sides and curl the ends by rolling them horizontally around a small-barreled curling iron. ⊖

9 Unclip the front and dress some over the beehive. Sweep the rest to the side and pin underneath. ➡

PRO TIP

Curling the ends of the hair makes it easier to manipulate them when tucking them over the hair pad.

Swinging sixties

YOU WILL NEED

- → Water
- → Hair brush
- → Heated rollers
- → Roller clips
- → Tail comb
- → Hairspray

1 Spritz dry hair lightly with water and brush through. →

3 Set the hair on heated rollers, starting at the top of the head. Clip each roller into place, using larger sized rollers on the top of the head. ←

2 Use a tail comb to create a deep side part. →

4 Use smaller rollers at the side, working downward and then around to the back of the head. Leave the rollers in until they are cold (about fifteen minutes). Spray lightly with hairspray. ⊖

5 When they are cool, gently unroll the rollers. As you unroll each section, lightly backcomb the root and spray with hairspray. ➜

6 Work through the hair across the whole head with the tail end of a tail comb to lift the hair at the roots and add volume. Spray to set. ⬇

PRO TIP

Plan your style carefully before you start working with rollers. The direction in which they are laid will dictate the fall of the hair. Rollers are used for volume and to give shape at the root.

1970s disco

YOU WILL NEED

- ➔ Sectioning clips
- ➔ Heated rollers
- ➔ Hairspray
- ➔ Hair straighteners
- ➔ Tail comb
- ➔ Bobby pins

1 Create a center part with a tail comb. Divide the hair into sections and clip, separating the hair closest to the forehead. ➔

3 Spray with hairspray and leave the rollers to cool for fifteen minutes. ➔

2 Set the hair on large, heated rollers, and make two pin curls with the hair at the front, securing with bobby pins. ➔

5 Unwind the front two pin curls and, using straighteners, curl them outward into flicks. ⬇

4 Remove the rollers (leaving the two front sections in their curls) and comb through the curls gently with your fingers. ⬆

6 Gently tease the ends of the curls individually to create volume. ⬅

7 Spray with hairspray to set. ⊘

PRO TIP

Creating a zig-zag part will add extra volume to this look.

1980s power dressing

YOU WILL NEED

- ➔ Heated rollers
- ➔ Hairpins
- ➔ Hairdryer
- ➔ Tail comb
- ➔ Hairspray

1 Set the hair on heated rollers. Starting at the front of the head, apply a line of small- to medium-sized rollers from ear to ear across the forehead. As you lift a length of hair to put a roller in, spray with hairspray before rolling down to the root. The section of hair on each roller should be as wide as the roller itself. ➔

3 Leave for 10–15 minutes, then remove the rollers. ➔

2 After inserting rollers, spray the whole head with hairspray and blast with the hairdryer for a few minutes so the hair takes the shape of the rollers. ➔

4 As you take each roller out, lightly backcomb the ends of the hair to tease it into a fluffy shape. Spray with hairspray and move on to the next roller. ⬆

5 Fluff up all the hair by lightly backcombing the ends toward the root with a big, sweeping stroke. ⬆

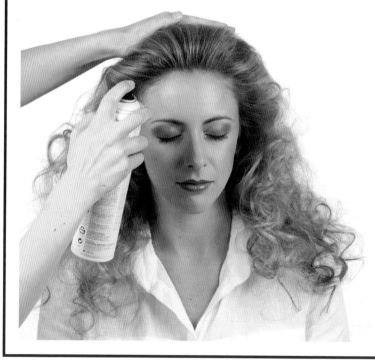

6 With the comb, smooth the hair around the forehead away from the face, and spray with hairspray, then smooth it over with a tail comb to get a tidy style. ↩

PRO TIP

Rollers are used here for added volme.
Varying the size of the rollers will vary
the height of the style.

1980s men's fashion

YOU WILL NEED

- → Thin ceramic straighteners
- → Thin tail comb
- → Hair grips
- → Hair extensions (as necessary)
- → Scissors
- → Wax
- → Hairspray
- → Toupee clips

1 Comb through the model's hair and straighten all over. ↷

2 More length can be added with a strip of hair extension fixed in with toupee clips sewn into the top seam, or gripped with bobby pins. Lift the hair and make a straight line with a tail comb. ↷

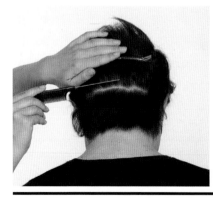

3 Backcomb the hair lightly and spray where the clip is to sit so that it grips in place. →

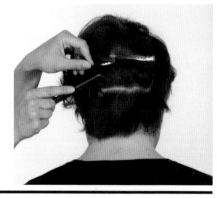

4 Fix the extension in place and comb the model's own hair over it to conceal. ⬆

5 Trim the extension to the desired length, keeping with the cut of the model's own hair. ⬇

6 Apply a small amount of wax or gel to the sides and comb away from the face horizontally with the fingers. Spray in place. ⬆

7 Unclip the top section and dress the hair in place with a comb. Create a side part with the tail of a tail comb and backcomb the roots for lift. ⬆

PRO TIP

If your model has short hair and you use a hair extension, make sure it is similar to your model's own hair in texture, and identical in color. You may have to dye it so it matches.

1980s girls' fashion

YOU WILL NEED

- ➲ Sectioning clips
- ➲ Styling mousse
- ➲ Paddle brush
- ➲ Hairbrush
- ➲ Crimpers
- ➲ Hairspray
- ➲ Spray wax
- ➲ Bobby pins

1 Section the hair (see page 16). ⬇

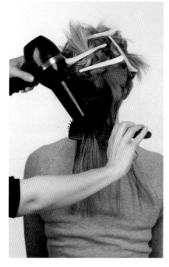

2 Starting at the nape of the neck, unclip the sections one at a time. Work a small amount of mousse into each section and blow-dry, using a flat paddle brush. ⬆

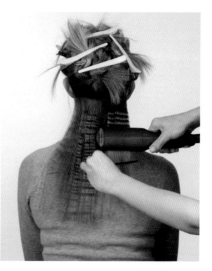

3 Crimp each section of the hair individually (see page 18) before unclipping the next part. ⬅

PRO TIP

Crimpers should be squeezed tightly to make sure the hair is crimping between the plates.

4 Spray through the hair with spray wax or texturizing spray. ➔

5 Turn the head upside down. Shake out the hair, and separate any clumps with your fingers. Mist all over with hairspray. ➔

6 Turn the head up the right way. To add extra length, attach sections of extra hair (see page 22) close to the head with bobby pins. ➔

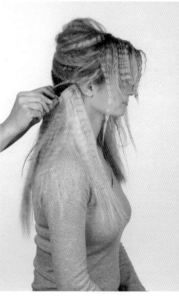

1990s glamour

YOU WILL NEED

- Sectioning clips
- Tail comb
- Finishing cream
- Hairspray
- Water

1 Spritz the hair with water. ⬆

2 Make an off-center part to the left, with the arm of a tail comb. ⬆

3 Split the hair into sections for blow-drying (see page 16). Start to blow-dry the hair, working from the nape of the neck upward. Angle the dryer down the shaft of hair and away from the head, pulling the hair firmly away from the head. Scoop the hair over the top of a round brush while drying. ➡

4 Work on each section individually until it is dry. You will need to pull very firmly if the hair is wavy or curly. As you move up through the sections toward the top of the head, begin to lift the hair at the root. ⬇

5 When you reach the top section, roll the hair round the brush and roll it down to the scalp while drying. ⬆

6 Create a soft inward curl at the end of the hair by rolling the ends back over the brush. ↩

7 If required, straighten through the top section to get a finished look. Rub finishing cream between your fingers, and lightly glaze over the hair. Spray with hairspray to finish. ⊖

PRO TIP

If your model's hair is fragile, use a low setting on the iron. If it's thick and unruly, make the heat almost the hottest it can be. When in doubt, keep it on a lower setting; it will be less damaging.

1990s grunge

YOU WILL NEED

- Water
- Mousse or styling lotion
- Comb
- Sectioning clips
- Small, round brush
- Hairspray

1 Damp the hair down with water spray. Protect the clothing with a towel and make sure the water is lukewarm. ➔

2 Work mousse or styling lotion into the hair and comb it through with your fingers. ⬅

3 Section off the top part of the hair and clip it out of the way. ➔

4 Blow-dry the hair, starting at the bottom and angling the hot air downward. Pull the hair away from the head and downward as you blow-dry. ➔

5 When blow-drying the tips of the hair, lift the hair from underneath with a medium roller brush, and dry from the root to the ends. Hold the dryer above the length of hair you are drying, angling the nozzle down toward the hair. ⬇

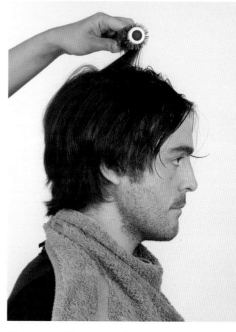

6 To create lift on top, pull the hair forward at a 45-degree angle as you dry. ⬆

7 Make a center part. Create lift on the forehead and a flick on each side of the head by rolling the hair as far as the root round a round brush. As you unroll the hair, scoop the brush down toward the hair until it is vertical. ⬇

8 Dress the hair into place with a comb and spray to hold. ⬆

PRO TIP

When used with a hairdryer, a small, round brush is good for creating waves, whereas a large-diameter, round brush is better at straightening and smoothing the hair. This look is quite natural and messy, which is why we have chosen to use the small brush.

CREDITS

All studio photographs are by Martin Norris, © Quintet Publishing.

Shutterstock images appear on the following pages: 1, 2, 6, 7, 10, 11, 12, 13, 15, 28

Quintet Publishing wishes to thank The Kobal Collection for its picture research, and permission to use the photographs for the Gallery section of the book.

The Kobal Collection owes its existence to the vision, courage, talent and energy of the men and women who created the movie industry and whose legacies live on through the films they made, the studios they built, and the publicity photographs they took. Kobal collects, preserves, organizes and makes these photographs available.

Kobal and Quintet Publishing wish to thank all the film distribution and production companies listed below whose publicity stills appear in this book. The publishers apologize in advance for any omissions, and would be pleased to make any necessary changes in future editions.

a = *above*, b = *below*, l = *left*, r = *right*, c = *centre*, t = *top*, f = *far*

P2: l. 20th Century Fox, cl. Universal, cr. Orion, r. Icon /Ladd Co / Paramount; P3: l. Studio Canal / Working Title / Sparham, Laurie, cl. cr. Warner Bros / Bailey, Alex; P4: from top. Icon Ent / Buena Vista, MGM, Warner Bros, Weinstein Co / Bailey, Alex, Universal / James, David, 20th Century Fox / Powolny, Frank; P26: Studio Canal; P27: fl. Tri Star, l. Touch Stone / Universal, c. Warner Bros, fr. Warner Bros tv / Bright / Kauffman / Crane Pro / Jones, Sam; P28: c. Warner Bros / Halstead, Dirck; P29: at. Universal, al. Universal, ac. Enigma / Goldcrest / BSB / Appleby, David, ar. ICC / Cine-trail, bt. Universal / Robert

Stigwood, bl. Paramount, bc. De Laurentiis / 20th Century Fox, br. Paramount; P30: at. Warner Bros / Bailey, Alex, al. Warner Bros, ac. MGM, ar. Warner Bros / Bailey, Alex, bt. 20th Century Fox, bl. MGM, bc. Dreamworks / Universal / Buitendijk, Japp, br. Dreamworks / Universal / Buitendijk, Japp; P31: at. Icon Ent /Buena Vista, al. Icon Ent /Buena Vista, ac. Icon Ent/Buena Vista / Cooper, Andrew, ar. Icon Ent /Buena Vista, bt. 20th Century Fox, bl. United Artists, bc. Kinofabrika / X-Filme, br. Beijing Film Studio; P32: at. Icon / Ladd Co / Paramount / Blanshard, Richard (N), al. Icon / Ladd Co / Paramount, ac. Icon / Ladd Co /

Paramount, ar. Icon / Ladd Co / Paramount, bt. Sony Pictures Classics / Braun, Steve, bl. Premier Heure / Schlemmer / France 3, bc. Paramount; P33: at. Miramax Films / Universal Pictures / Sparham, Laurie, al. Studio Canal / Working Title / Sparham, Laurie, ac. Studio Canal / Working Title / Sparham, Laurie, ar. Studio Canal / Working Title / Williams, Greg, bt. British and Dominions, bl. Columbia / Irving Allen, bc. Paramount, br. 20th Century Fox; P34: at. Warner Bros, al. Ikiru Films SL / Dreamworks SKG, ac. Merchant Ivory, ar. Merchant Ivory, bt. Les Films Ariane / Filmsonor / Vides, bl. Touchstone / Buena Vista Pictures, bc. Warner Bros, br. Hanway

/ Medusa / RPC; P35: at. Focus Features, al. Pioneer Pictures / Bachrach, Ernest, ac. Working Title, ar. MGM, bt. MGM, bl. Paramount, bc. MGM / Bull, Clarence Sinclair, br. Paramount; P36: at. Warner Bros, al. MGM / Willinger, Laszlo, ac. Alcon Entertainment / Close, Murray, ar. Columbia / Pathe / Sony, bt. Warner Bros, bl. Warner Bros, bc. Kiru Films SL / Dreamworks SKG, br. Griffith / United Artists; P37: at. Hook Prods / Amblin, al. Walt Disney / Mountain, Peter, ac. Walt Disney, ar. 20th Century Fox, bt. Warner Bros, bl. Columbia, bc. RKO / Bachrach, Ernest, br. Stanley Kramer / United Artists; P38: at. 20th Century Fox / Universal, al.

Scott Free / Enigma / Paramount, ac. United Artists, ar. Warner Bros, bt. Columbia, bl. Weinstein Co / Bailey, Alex, bc. MGM / Bull, Clarence Sinclair, br. MGM; P39: at. Miramax / Dimension Films / Chedlow, Paul, ac. 20th Century Fox, ar. Samuel Bronston, bt. British Lion, bl. Icon / Pathe / Bailey, Alex, bc. MGM, br. MGM; P40: at. Romulus / Warwick, al. Dreamworks / Warner Bros / Mountain, Peter, ac. CBS, ar. Paramount, bt. MGM, bl. Turner / New Line, bc. Turner / New Line, br. Tri Star; P41: at. Di Novi / Columbia, al. Selznick / MGM, ac. Selznick / MGM, ar. Miramax, bt. 20th Century Fox, bl. Universal, bc. 20th Century Fox, br. Orion; P42: at. Bandai Visual / Dentsu Inc., al. Paramount / Dyar, Otto, ac. Paramount, ar. Columbia / Michaels, Darren, bt. Associated British, bl. 20th Century Fox / Paramount, bc. Walt Disney Pictures, br. Merchant Ivory; P43: at. Hesser, Edwin Bower, ar. Metro, bt. Wardour, bl. Paramount, bc. Miramax / James, David, br. United Artists; P44: at. United Artists, al. Universal, ac. 20th Century Fox, ar. Touchstone / Universal, bt. MGM / Hurrell, George,

bc. United Artists, br. MGM / Bull, Clarence Sinclair; P45: al. Hurrell, George, bt. Gainsborough, br. MGM; P46: at. MGM, al. Universal / James, David, ac. 20th Century Fox, ar. Focus Features / Bailey, Alex, bl. Universal, br. Columbia / Coburn, Bob; P47: at. Warner Bros / Halstead, Dirck, al. Paramount, ac. Warner Bros / First National / Welbourne, Scotty, ar. 20th Century Fox, br. 29th Century Fox; P48: at. MGM, al. 20th Century Fox, ac. MGM / Bull, Clarence Sinclair, ar. 20th Century Fox, bc. CBS-TV, br. Warner Bros; P49: at. MGM, al. Paramount, ac. 20th Century Fox, ar. Warner Bros, bt. MGM, bc. Paramount; P50: at. Warner Bros, al. New Line / James, David, ac. New Line / James, David, ar. United Artists, bt. Paramount, bl. MGM, bc. Dreamworks / James, David, br. New Line / Wright, K; P51: al. Spelling-Goldberg / Costa, Tony, ac. Warner Bros, ar. ABC, bt. 20th Century Fox, bc. Gladden Entertainment, br. Columbia Pictures / Embassy Pictures; P52: at. Baywatch Co / Tower 12 Prods, al. Costa, Tony, ac. Paramount, ar. Paramount, bt. Universal, bl. Orion, bc.

Touchstone, br. MGM; P53: at. Warner Bros, al. Warner Bros Tv / Bright / Kauffman / Crane Pro / Jones, Sam, ac. Anarchy Prods / D'Alema, Guy, ar. Fox, Uchitel, Diego, bt. Morgan Creek / Davis Films, bl. Columbia TV, bc. Jersey Films / Redin, Van, br. 20th Century Fox; P55: Universal; P58: Paramount; P63: Warner Bros; P66: MGM; P71: Icon Ent / Buena Vista; P74: United Artists; P79: Icon / Ladd Co / Paramount; P82: Premiere Heure / Schlemmer / France 3; P87: Studio Canal / Working Title / Sparham, Laurie; P90: Columbia / Irving Allen; P95: Ikiru Films SL / Dreamworks SKG; P98: Touchstone / Buena Vista Pictures; P103: Pioneer Pictures / Bachrach, Ernest; P106: Paramount; P111: MGM / Willinger, Laszlo; P114: Warner Bros; P119: Walt Disney / Mountain, Peter; P122: Columbia; P127: Scott Free / Enigma / Paramount; P131: Weinstein Co / Bailey, Alex; P139: Icon / Pathe / Bailey, Alex; P143: Dreamworks / Warner Bros / Mountain, Peter; P147: Turner / New Line; P151: Selznick / MGM; P155: Universal; P159: Paramount / Dyar, Otto; P163: 20th Century Fox / Paramount

/ Wallace, Merie W; P171: Paramount / Richee, E.R; P175: Universal; P183: Hurrell, George; P191: Universal / James, David; P195: Universal; P199: Paramount; P207: 20th Century Fox; P215: Paramount; P223: New Line / James, David; P227: MGM; P230: Spelling-Goldberg / Costa, Tony; P239: Costa, Tony; P243: Touchstone; P247: Warner Bros TV / Bright / Kaufman / Crane Pro / Jones, Sam; P251: Columbia TV

INDEX